Seed Saving

Create a Seed Bank to Become Self-sufficient

(The Complete Guide to Store, Preserve and Harvest the Seeds From Your Favorite Fruits)

Doyle Duenas

Published By **John Kembrey**

Doyle Duenas

All Rights Reserved

Seed Saving: Create a Seed Bank to Become Self-sufficient (The Complete Guide to Store, Preserve and Harvest the Seeds From Your Favorite Fruits)

ISBN 978-0-9959965-8-8

No part of this guidebook shall be reproduced in any form without permission in writing from the publisher except in the case of brief quotations embodied in critical articles or reviews.

Legal & Disclaimer

The information contained in this book is not designed to replace or take the place of any form of medicine or professional medical advice. The information in this book has been provided for educational & entertainment purposes only.

The information contained in this book has been compiled from sources deemed reliable, and it is accurate to the best of the Author's knowledge; however, the Author cannot guarantee its accuracy and validity and cannot be held liable for any errors or omissions. Changes are periodically made to this book. You must consult your doctor or get professional medical advice before using any of the suggested remedies, techniques, or information in this book.

Upon using the information contained in this book, you agree to hold harmless the Author from and against any damages, costs, and expenses, including any legal fees potentially resulting from the application of any of the information provided by this guide. This disclaimer applies to any damages or injury caused by the use and application, whether directly or indirectly, of any advice or information presented, whether for breach of contract, tort, negligence, personal injury, criminal intent, or under any other cause of action.

You agree to accept all risks of using the information presented inside this book. You need to consult a professional medical practitioner in order to ensure you are both able and healthy enough to participate in this program.

Table Of Contents

Chapter 1: What Are Survival Seeds? 1

Chapter 2: The Bees Disease 21

Chapter 3: Finding The Right Seeds 35

Chapter 4: Sunlight And Shade 62

Chapter 5: Putting It All Together 84

Chapter 6: Keep Seeds Cool 105

Chapter 7: The Complete Guide To Growing And Storing Vegetables, Fruits, Herbs 111

Chapter 8: How To Grow Vegetables In Winter 130

Chapter 9: How To Grow Vegetables In Containers 144

Chapter 10: Common Vegetable Gardening Problems 156

Chapter 11: Important Tools That Are Useful For Vegetable Gardening 171

Chapter 1: What Are Survival Seeds?

Imagine, for a moment the scenario of an emergency that lasts for a long time. There will be a discussion of the actual threats to the supply of food in the next chapter but in the meantime it's enough to say that there was a traumatic event that shut your access to the comforts of life in the modern world. No food, no water, no electricity, nothing. Everything you've come to expect on your list are readily offered.

You don't have to be worried, say you You're stocked with water and food available within the cellar. The house is stocked with guns and ammo to safeguard your family members as well as a fairly secluded portion of land. It's likely that order will soon be restored and the property will be restored to normal. So, sit back and watch while keeping an eye on.

The weeks pass by and then you're left with no news. They change into months. Within a quarter of a year it becomes apparent that you're completely on your own. Food security that was once plentiful hasn't been as useful as it was in the past, and you're left trying to determine what to do if your supplies for emergencies are exhausted.

What do you do if have run out of food?

The shelves of stores will be empty and that's not no way to go. It's not possible to purchase a fresh supply of food items from Amazon. Any food source in the vicinity of a mile was tapped and sanitized months ago. There must be a backup plan, and it must have a longer-term emergency strategy. Instead of having just food items, you'll have to find a way of creating food.

If you have survival seeds and you've got the means to produce the food you need. It's important to think ahead and begin to grow it prior to running out of food for emergencies, but if you get started early with your food production and you have a sustainable energy source.

In the absence of any survival seeds, you'll need to believe that luck is at your back. It will be a challenge to find food as everyone and their mom is looking for exactly what as you. The only way to find food is to gather and hunt but if you don't succeed then you'll need to venture into cities to look to find foods. If you are able to find food it is best to battle for it as there'll be other seeking the same scraps.

The best way to live is in the event that you've traveled in a remote area and has the plants for living off the soil. The fewer hours you're required to be in close proximity to civilization is the better. It is likely that civilization will turn into an extremely uncivilized area when there is a prolonged emergency.

If you're unsure regarding how dire the situation are going to get, check out videos of people calling for to protest after their EBT cards were shut down for a brief period of duration in the month of October 2013. This is a shocking glimpse into the mental state of those who are convinced that they'll need to survive without food.

In one video on the internet, a person from Los Angeles threatens chaos, declaring, "They better resolve something because if it stays like this, there's gonna be an uproar in the city of L.A." In one of the videos, a lot of Wal-Mart stores throughout the United States were hit by riots, and at least one Walmart was forced to close because customers started to become disruptive. This all happened when the store was shut off for just an hour. Imagine what could happen when people were left hungry for the whole month or more.

Survival seeds are the seeds that you keep to assure your existence.

They will permit the cultivation of crops for whatever you choose to keep within the seed vault. You'll be able to get away from the bustle of city life and begin a new one someplace far away from society.

If you can only recall only one thing you learned from the book, be sure to remember this.

There's no need to worry about what amount of food you've saved for emergency in case the situation of survival persists for a long time. It's inevitable that you'll be depleted of food. When you do, it's best to be able to create additional food. Start your collection of seeds for survival now and learning to cultivate the best ones is the most effective strategy to ensure your survival for the long haul.

Do not get me wrong. Do not forget the emergency stash of food, and focus instead on preserving survival seeds. It is likely that you will require food and also, however, stockpiled food can only provide you with a few days. Keep as much food in your pantry as you can. However, in addition to the food, it is also necessary to keep a stash of survival seeds.

Food you've saved is just an end in itself. It's a way to get there. It's your key to immediate survival, which will enable you to live until you can plant your seeds for survival and then grow to produce productive plants.

Real Threats to the Global Food Supply

When you think about the long-term scenario of survival What do you think of?

Most likely, you are thinking of possibilities like nuclear Armageddon huge asteroids crashing into Earth or one of the many possible apocalyptic scenarios Mother Nature can send at us. In reality, the chance of ever-increasing superstorms, massive volcanic eruptions, or even a planet-wide deep freeze is very slim. There's almost no likelihood that any of these scenarios can be achieved There are a variety of threats to our food supply that appear far more likely to be a reality.

Although apocalyptic scenarios make fantastic Hollywood films, the dangers I'm about to inform you about are real dangers you have to be worried about. Let me be real with you certain scenarios I'm going to discuss can be more terrifying than the threat of a nuclear explosion or an attack by a foreign force. These scenarios could result in global hungry people and even starvation all over the world. This isn't the time to panic right now, but it's the best time ever to prepare for the eventuality of survival.

The majority of people living in all of the Western world have enjoyed food in their reach. If you're in the market for a burger there are a variety of choices, ranging from McDonald's drive-through, to a sitting-down eatery to purchasing the fresh meat at the market and then making your own burger. If you're thirsty there are locations to buy drinks wherever there is a variety of drinking fountains with the option of free drinking water. No matter if you're looking for an ice cream or a complete dinner or anything else There's never a time where food isn't available that is within reach.

I often talk about survival as well as threat to our food supply and the response I receive from people is always sure to be awe-inspiring. The majority of people don't believe that the food they've grown used to won't remain available for the duration the time. The food has always been available which is why they have an assumption that it's going to be available. If presented with proof of actual threats most people dismiss menaces as being a form of an act of paranoia.

The remaining portion of this chapter focuses on various threats for the supply of food. If you're not up to date on this type of information expect to be stunned.

Remember that I only picked a small sample of the multitude of dangers that are currently threatening the food industry as well as in the U.S. and across the world.

A few of these dangers have a higher chance of being implemented than others. However, should any of them occurs, the effects on the supply of food could be disastrous.

Population Growth May Outpace Food Production

Over 7 billion people around the world at present. This is billion with the letter B. For a better understanding this would be enough people to fill 170,000 soccer stadiums. If the entire planet were to line up side-byside, there'd more than enough people to cover the Earth at least 100 times. This is quite a amount of people, and numbers are growing with leaps and upwards.

This hasn't always been the in the past.

Around 10,000 years ago, less than 5 million wandering around the Earth. The hunter and gatherer faced hardship and did not take much time to make and raising infants. The survival rate of infants was low due to the demands of living. When the population grew too large within a specific area there would be a shortage of food and the population could adjust to accommodate. It is no surprise that these were tough times.

The moment people realised that they did not need to wander the Earth to hunt for food, the world changed. Civilizations developed as individuals learned to manage the land, and also raise livestock. It was the Agricultural Revolution created a surplus of food that allowed people to survive off the soil like they had never before. Over the next 8000 years, and the global population increasing from 5 million at 8000 BC up to 200 million to 600 million in 1 AD.

The growth rate remained constant through the time that it was the time that Industrial

Revolution took place starting around 1760. The new manufacturing techniques allowed more food products to be made as the population of the world exploded and reached the one billion number in 1804. Although it took many millions of years increase to 1.01 billion, it only took more than 120 years to reach the 2nd billion mark in 1927. In less than 50 years for population to increase by 4 billion in 1974. We crossed 7 billion. In the past few years, growth rates have decreased somewhat, but the an average of 80 million per year have been added to the total, and there is a chance that we'll hit 8 billion in 2024. Then, 9 billion people by 2046.

So far, the globe is able to keep pace with the global food needs by providing enough food to millions of people through improvements in technology and improved ways to produce food. There are places in the world in which famine occurs, the vast majority of people can procure enough food for survival. Innovations in irrigation and farming technology, and the improvement of use of pesticides and herbicides in the production of food have enabled farmers around the world to expand their farming areas and increase the quantity of food they produce on their farms to satisfy the growing demands of humanity.

The issue with this kind of development is that it could not last long. Farmer's ability to feed all of people on Earth could not last long since the numbers continue to rise and it's already beginning to slip behind in a few areas. There over 90 countries around the world with in a shortage of food and aren't producing enough food that they require to provide for their population.

The world may look fine however, we've been operating with borrowed time from the 1970's when mankind surpassed something referred to as Earth's biocapacity. It's the capacity of the Earth to regenerate its biological resources while that they are being utilized, and taking in the garbage that we produce. Simply put that the Earth can't maintain the current population for the long term, not to mention those who are pumping into it each year.

Already, we're seeing the consequences of the overpopulation crisis in several regions around the globe. Based on data of the Food and Agriculture Organization from 2013 there were nearly 8 million people in the world who live without food frequently. We who are fortunate enough to reside somewhere in the Western world seldom see starving individuals outside of a rare advertisement on television or in a magazine as 98% reside in countries that are developing in Asia, Africa and Latin America. It's easy to close your at the rest of the world when their struggles aren't directly staring us directly in the face.

All over the world, people have to make do with the land which has been over-grazed and live in zones susceptible to flooding, droughts and other natural catastrophes that render it impossible to grow food. Some live in shacks or shanty towns in areas that aren't huge areas of population and have to beg for scraps of food.

There are people who live in unimaginable situations like those of children who live in Brazil, India and a several other emerging countries which are confined in filthy garbage pits which they use to spend their time exploring the trash for clothes, food scraps of food, and other recyclable materials that they are able to sell for $2 or so a day. The estimates suggest that around 4000 kids in Brazil alone are living in garbage dumps, and over one million residents are in India must go through garbage to make ends meet.

It is difficult to increase production in order to meet demands is insufficient. With the rapid growth of population growing, more and more regions in the world are expected to be left behind and start to experience hunger. Many experts predict the possibility of a global food crisis because crop yields don't seem to increase at an enough rate to keep pace with the growth in population.

In the near-term the growth in population isn't an immediate threat for those who live in the Western world, however it's something you should be on the lookout for. While you're waiting you could take a chance by learning how to cultivate yourself food as well as cultivate your own livestock. In the event that your food supplies begin to decrease it will be your own responsibility and possess an own supply of food.

Drought, Declining Rivers and Empty Aquifers: Are We Running Out of Water?

Let's make one thing crystal straight this moment. We will never end up without water as the water that we consume isn't able to leave the confines that are the Earth. Every drop of water used during the dinosaur's time on Earth remains in a form of some sort.

The issue we're facing in the present is that water isn't where we have to put it to be able to use it to produce food.

The population grows and food demand increases, we require ever more water in order for the production of food. This places a huge stress on our local water resources within the regions where the majority of our food crops are grown. Rivers that were once fast and dump hundreds of thousands of gallon liquid into the waters, bays and gulfs that they are connected to, now only a trickle until they make it to the ocean, should they're able to make it there at all. The year 2001 saw in 2001, the Rio Grande ran dry before it reached an ocean, for the first time in history.

The once-horrific rivers of California as well as the Mid-West have similar problems. The water is so extensively used to produce food and drink that they're essentially an insignificant stream when they get to the ocean. The problem is made worse due to the fact that most of California is regularly subject to droughts, while the snowpack has become only a tiny fraction of what used to be. A large portion of the population requires the water they consume for showers, pools, and lawns. There is also a shortage of water to the farmers who are responsible for cultivating crops.

California is currently in the middle of a drought which may result in the water supply cut off for a variety of farms within the next few years. At the time of writing this report, most of the largest reservoirs located in California are at or below 20% capacity and appear more like mud pits, than they are reservoirs. A lot of them run off of rivers which are dependent on snow runoff and snowpacks have not been as good for many years.

For the most part there are vast areas across America United States (and the world in general) are tapping into aquifers underground and are gradually taking them out of their water. The water in aquifers is replenished naturally after they rain and when snow melts, making use of the water they contain is not a problem until the point at which you're consuming much more water than it is actually entering the water aquifer.

The Ogallala Aquifer is a large part of Nebraska as well as portions of Kanas, Colorado, Oklahoma, New Mexico and Texas. It's the principal water source for large stretches across the Midwest and is depleting more quickly than it is replenished. The table of water within the Ogallala Aquifer is decreasing to as low as two feet a year in places where very little water gets into the Aquifer.

If we were to stop taking aquifers from today--and there is no way to do that because the agriculture in these regions provide us with about a fifth the wheat, corn and cattle as well as cotton that is utilized across America--it will take a long time for the aquifers to fill up.

The problem of depleted aquifers isn't that is only a problem in those in the United States. According to estimates, at least 18 countries are taking out water from their aquifers, but they don't replenish fast enough to replenish the amount of water that's being pulled from them. States like Saudi Arabia, Syria and Yemen have depleted their water sources until they have begun to dry up and they have to cut down on the production of crops for food like rice, wheat, and barley. As the world's the population is growing rapidly and the supply of water has been slashed to the point of being nothing.

It's possible that we're not in the process of running out of water across the planet, but we're getting water shortages in areas that matter the most. If we don't take action soon so that our farms can have adequate water in the near in the future, we'll be left on our own in the field of growing agricultural crops. The situation isn't in an emergency point however, something has to be done to ensure that water gets to those where it is needed.

Chapter 2: The Bees Disease

The number of bees currently in the world is declining across the world. About a third of all commercial colonies of bees are dying since. Scientists are attempting to discover the reason why bees have been dying in such rapid numbers and they have speculated that they are caused by the mites, a virus and global warming as well as pollution, and pesticides. There are many different theories.

No matter the reason the cause, the colony collapse disorder (CCD) is what it's dubbed and is causing the death of millions of bees every year. Over 10 million hives are completely gone when the disease was first discovered in the year 2006. Beekeepers throughout in the United States are reporting losing up to 90 percentage of their honeybees due in the course of CCD.

Bees are needed to help pollinate flowers which produce fruits and other vegetables. Without bees, crops will have to be pollinated manually and this isn't practical in the amount that is required to feed people in the millions. Bees aren't here and it's already affecting the world's food supply and the situation could be more severe if the dying off continues.

As an indicator of what is to follow, Californian almond farmers are finding it difficult to obtain the bees needed to grow bumper almond crop. California's almond production is the largest in the world, producing 80percent of the almonds it produces. A trip through I-5 in California will reveal many acres of almonds stretching as much as one can imagine. The area doesn't have a sufficient number of natural bees living that live in the area to provide the many orchards. So, farmers have to bring into hives from across the nation. Farmers recently contacted for delivery of bees, similar to what they've been doing since the beginning of time and have been doing for a long time, they discovered that the beekeepers who they usually use weren't in a position to provide the necessary hives.

Farmers were fortunate and could scramble to find the hives they wanted, but should the global decline in bees is not stopped and the almond business continues to decline, it could slow down as well as a variety of other businesses that depend on bees.

Here are some of the plants that rely on honeybees to pollinate:

* Alfalfa.

* Apples.

* Blueberries.

* Boysenberries.

* Brazil nuts.

* Broccoli.

* Cactus.

* Carrots.

* Cherries.

* Clover.

* Cotton.

* Cranberries.

* Eggplant.

* Figs.

* Grapes.

* Lemons.

* Limes.

* Onions.

* Nectarines and peaches.

* Sunflower.

* Tomatoes.

* Watermelon.

* Plus there are many more.

It's quite amazing, and somewhat scary to realize the extent to which our agricultural products depend on the dwindling honeybee number. Certain crops may be pollinated in a small amount by other insects flying around but not at the amount they get when honeybees exist, specifically those areas where honeybees have been brought to farms to help ensure pollination.

Without bees there'll not be much produce available that can be found in the stores. Prices will rise in comparison to what's available, and it's best to know how to cultivate (and help pollinate) yourself your food, or you'll find yourself in deep, serious trouble.

Phosphate Supplies Are Dwindling

Large-scale agriculture rely on phosphate fertilizers for growing plants. This can be problematic since the phosphate resource is limited which is being extracted underground at record amounts. The supply of phosphate is decreasing and some experts believe that we'll reach peak phosphate in the coming 20 years.

When one of the peak phosphate levels is reached when this vital fertilizer component will be scarce, and the remaining phosphate to be extracted will turn out exorbitantly costly. What happens after that is a mystery, however the possibility of food shortages, and massive rises in prices of food is a real possibility. There is also the possibility that huge populations will be left to fend on their own and massive food insecurity could happen. A certain specialist has been quoted saying that the number of people on the Earth may be cut to as low as 1.5 billion when the phosphate supply is dwindling down.

This is compounded by the issue that China has the largest share of global phosphate supplies. Although there is a chance that U.S. does have some naturally occurring phosphorus, its reserves are expected to run empty in around 15 years. This puts us at fate of China, Morocco and the small number of countries who are still producing the phosphorus. The cost of phosphorus is expected to rise, and with food prices if it is the case that U.S. isn't able to find a new way to create the phosphorus.

Interestingly enough, despite the fact that it is predicted that phosphorus will run out within the next few years however, we're exporting massive quantities of it to China. When our supply decreases and we're forced to look towards the rest of the world to buy our Phosphorus, I'm not sure China is as nimble of phosphorus remaining as they are with ours.

Farmers will have to pay higher rates for phosphorus. This will affect our food supply in various ways. The farmers will be using less phosphorus which will produce lower yields. Lower yields can cause a rise in the cost of food and, eventually the average household might not be able be able to afford food for the family. In this case, you can expect an array of chaos to follow.

The hope doesn't end for now, because scientists may be able to discover a way to get phosphorus out of the fecal and urine matter yet, to date, no one has yet come up with an efficient and cost-effective technique that can be employed to extract sufficient Phosphorus to have a positive impact.

Over-Farming: When Will the Land Give Out?

In all over the world regions of natural vegetation are being cleared so that arable land can be exposed on which crops could be grown. Farmers plough this land in order for the purpose of planting plants. They then turn the land under and then plough it back. Then again. Then again. Again.

The process of planting and plowing can be hard on the land. If you've been on an agricultural property when the fields are being ploughed then you've likely observed the massive puffs of dust that rise up in the vicinity of the tractor. It's topsoil, and the majority of it blows off to settle on the four corners of Earth. In time, this can lead to fertile soil that's no longer suitable for farming like it used to be.

Though a small amount of dust blowing around might appear small but it's believed that a third of arable land across the globe is ruined by excessive farming and erosion since the 1960's. Since vast tracts of land disappear from farming Farmers move onto larger areas nearby, causing damage to areas that are to be used up. In the end farmers will have no land they can move into and be forced to work with the land they have.

Although the soil may not be disappearing, farmers frequently utilize unsustainable methods of farming that eliminate carbon permanently out of the soil, causing salt to accumulate within the topsoil. The highly industrialized zones release chemicals into groundwater, which further reduces the soil. Pesticides and herbicides cause a buildup and make the soil infertile.

The degraded soil can cause the declining water supply that was mentioned earlier because soil that is degraded can't hold in the water like healthy soil. The topsoil is able to hold water for longer and allows the plant's roots to soak it up. It is a fact that water flows right through damaged soil, and the majority is going to drain directly past the plant's roots. The result is a higher demands for water, at the time that water conservation might be essential to the survival of our species.

Given that it can take years for soil that has been degraded to regenerate, something must be done right now, since huge areas of land are becoming inaccessible.

Heirloom Seeds and Why They're Important

Another thing I did not touch in the last section is the direction in which the agriculture industry is heading regarding the seeds that are used in the production of crop. The seeds are a serious danger to food security. To better understand why these seeds could cause a major disruption to food production we must first examine the types of seeds that are commonly used that are available today.

Seed types include:

* Hybrid seed.

* Seeds that have been genetically altered.

* Seeds that are open-pollinated and heirloom.

Three types of seeds are produced similarly. They're either sown in the soil and then grown, or sprouted, and later placed in the soil. All of them grow into plants that yield a certain variety of crops.

Pollinated openly by birds, insects and wind, and often they're even given an aid by human beings trying to make sure they're being pollinated by the correct sort of pollen. When butterflies, bees, Hummingbirds, and various other species of insects fly from flower to flower pollen is absorbed by their bodies and legs.

If they take flight to a different species of flower or plant, this pollen dislodges from their bodies, and then pollinates the flowers that they come across. If plants germinate, they trigger a sequence of actions that eventually results in the growth of fruits or veggies. In the absence of pollination, flowers won't blossom, however there is no way for a fruit or vegetable to emerge from the bloom.

The open-pollinated plant is genetically diverse due to the uncertainty regarding the kind of pollen supplied into the plants. As time passes, the plants adjust to the climate where they're grown and new species of plants emerge. So long as proper the proper care is taken to make sure that no pollen of other species of that are of the same species is transferred to the crop that is open-pollinated, the kind of seeds created by open pollinated plants is true to type, which means they will grow the same plants or even larger bigger and stronger than their parents.

Selective breeding permits you to cultivate plants that have traits that you want. Through only pollinating varieties with desirable traits and characteristics, you are able to develop new species of plants during an the course of a long period of time.

Heirloom plants are open-pollinated varieties that have been selectedly bred for several years in order to produce specific characteristics unique to the particular type of plant. That's where the fascinating and stunning varieties of vegetables such as purple tomatoes and carrots with a swath of color running throughout them are derived from. They can see this in their plants and are able to breed plants with the same characteristics. As time passes, new kinds of plants emerge. Many believe that the heirloom plant needs been handed over for 50 to 100 years before they can be classified as an heirloom plant, however to simplify things we'll say that any plant that has been handed through multiple generations is considered as an heirloom.

The produce grown using local varieties of heirloom seeds usually tastes better and is more durable due to their ability to thrive in the climate prevalent in the area. When gardeners begin to switch to family-owned seeds, they don't go back and put all other varieties of seeds to the side for the more superior varieties of heirloom available.

Chapter 3: Finding The Right Seeds

There are many aspects you should be aware of when selecting plants for survival.

The weather, soil conditions and the amount of sunlight in the region you're planning to grow the seeds must be considered and so do the varieties of plants you're thinking about developing and the duration it will take to cultivate the seeds.

In addition, be sure to get your seeds from trusted sources, and recognize what kind of seeds that you're purchasing. The wrong kind of seeds or settling for inferior seeds that aren't fertile can have disastrous results when you're depending on them to survive.

Select the best seeds, and you'll be amazed at how easy they are to establish and grow well after being placed in the right place. Select the wrong seeds and you'll have to fight uphill all the duration.

What You Need to Know About Hardiness Zones

The environment you're cultivating plants in can make a massive distinction in the kinds of plants that you'll be able to grow successfully. The kind of plants that you'll be likely to see in the mountains of Colorado are completely different than the ones you're able to cultivate within Southern California.

To help that the people pick the appropriate species for their particular area To help people choose the best plants for their environment, to help people choose the right plants for their area, United States Department of Agriculture is dividing parts of U.S. into areas known as the Hardiness Zones. The Hardiness Zones are defined based on what is the lowest temperature a region is exposed to, typically in the middle of winter.

Many websites selling seeds online list the zones in which they can grow in. If you're purchasing seeds from a brick & mortar shop, the information must be included on the seeds' packet. When purchasing heirloom seeds through the farmer's market or private seller, you'll need be sure that they are suited to the conditions you have in. If you're purchasing seeds locally, and the plants are grown in the local area, this should be all the evidence you need.

There are twenty zones in total with each zone having an inclination of ten degrees in temperatures. The people who live in the climate zone 1, that is the coldest could experience temperatures as low as -50 degrees F. Contrastingly the climate zone 11 which is hottest, is characterized by temperatures in excess of 40deg F. Zones in between zone 1 and 11, are divided into two distinct zones with five degrees variances between low temperatures. As an example, 2a encompasses the range of -45deg F up to -50deg and zone 2b encompasses the range of -40deg F up to -45deg.

Below is a map showing the climate zones that are different:

This is a closer view of the key used identify the map

The map is a bit hard to comprehend, and especially in the black-and-white version printed in the book. Below is a URL to access the Online USDA Plant Hardiness Zone Map:

When you've identified the is the climate zone, or hardiness zone you're in and what zone you're in, you can utilize it to decide on the kinds of seeds you'd like to plant. The Hardiness zone temperature is a representation of the extreme cold winter temperatures that occur in the region. If you're seeking plants are able to grow during the winter months or can be kept in the ground then you must be aware of the zones of hardiness. Zones.

Utilizing Hardiness Zones by themselves to decide suitable seeds to plant has some drawbacks. They don't take winter high temperature, winter snow humidity or other variables into the equation. This could result in mixed outcomes when choosing seeds based solely on their hardiness. It is important to note that the Eastern United States is relatively flat, which is why the Hardiness Zones are a good fit. If you're moving to the west, you'll need to think about altitude because some plants can't thrive at higher elevations.

In case you're unsure, make contact with the seller to determine whether certain varieties are suitable to your region. They will be able to provide you with a good suggestion of the best time and place the seeds will be able to grow.

Hardiness Zones need to be considered in deciding which seeds to plant, however they shouldn't be the primary aspect to consider. Produce production requires much more than monitoring the Hardiness Zone before plant seeds in the soil.

Hardiness Zone 1

Low Temperature: Below -50deg F.

A typical Growing Season is 30 days.

Last Frost: Middle of June.

First Frost: Middle of July.

Information:

In light of the extreme cold temperatures as well as the severe conditions that accompany these temperatures which are common in the region, the it is said that the Hardiness Zone 1 is one of the areas that are most difficult for growing plants around the globe. Certain plants are able to grow outside, however you'll need to set your greenhouse or alternative location where you could plant plants with less severe circumstances. A different option is to plant plants in pots that can be wheeled both inside and out when the weather permits.

There's a chance that you can grow crops that thrive in Zones 2 and possibly 3. However, you'll need be required to keep an eye out for extreme storms that could destroy the plant. Plants that are annual are likely to be your best option, because there's no chances of the majority of crops being able to survive winter.

The season of growth is very short in Zone 1 and runs for a few months in the middle of season, which means that long-season crops are not feasible. Pick short-season, cold-hardy crops to get the optimal results.

What to Grow:

The only plant species that can are able to survive winter's severe conditions that are a part of Hardiness Zone 1 are a tiny number of woody stem plant species. There aren't any fruit or veggies that could be successfully able to survive the winter months in Zone 1. The best way to do this is to plant the seeds inside and then plant them once you have had the last frost.

Many vegetables work well in zones of hardiness 3 or higher. It is possible to select some plants from Zone 3 to develop during the shortened season of growth in Zone 1 but one or two days of extremely cold temperatures during the time of harvest could wipe out the whole plant.

If you are in Zone 1 then your best choice is to create an indoor greenhouse, and then learn you can use it for your benefit. Alternately, you could begin exploring Zone 2 or Zone 3 plants right now to determine how you'll be able to successfully cultivate one of these. Make sure you plan to weather the harsh winter months. Even if you manage to get through the frozen soil, there is no way to develop during wintertime in Zone 1. The survival gardening zone will require the cultivation of a large amount of food throughout the brief period of time and then putting enough food on the table for the winter to last.

To determine which is the most suitable crop to cultivate in Zone 1 In order to determine the best produce for Zone 1, you'll need to consider the amount of frost-free days that you can count on in the zone in which you reside and then examine the growing season for the product that you're planning to grow. If you have only 50 frost-free days, and you're thinking of trying to cultivate the vegetable you want to grow that needs 75 days of growth then you'll need begin your plants indoors before moving them outdoors following the end of frost.

The issue with growing outside in this area is that it is possible for frost to strike anytime and, if it happens occur, it will ruin a whole harvest. You can grow vegetables such as leeks, cabbage and kale which are tolerant of frost, however know that temperatures of extreme cold will nevertheless cause death to them.

Another issue you could encounter is ice on the ground. If permafrost is present in the location you're in It will be hard to plant something. It's possible to grow in containers or raised beds however, it's an uphill struggle.

Hardiness Zone 2

Low Temperature: -40deg F to -50deg F.

A typical Growing Season is 3 months.

Last Frost: Middle of May.

First Frost: Middle of August.

Information:

Zone 2 is yet another zone that is characterized by extremely cold temperatures, however it's not as frigid as Zone 1. There's a small selection of varieties of vegetables that could be planted in Zone

2, however, you'll be able to have greater options than Zone 1.

Like Zone 1, a greenhouse is a viable choice because it will allow you to extend your growing time a bit.

What to Grow:

The severe cold of Zone 2 prevents the growth of almost all fruit. Certain people have claimed that they've successfully produced Nanking Bush Cherries in Zone 2 but that is not proven. Regarding vegetables it is possible to plant various varieties of cabbage and potatoes in the tiniest period of growth, however extreme cold temperatures pose a worry. There are some who have had success with types of broccoli that are cold-hardy as well as cauliflower, kale, and onions.

Like the case with Zone 1 there is a chance that you'll have the ability to cultivate crops that is suitable for other zones over the brief summer time. It is necessary to begin most plant species indoors before transferring them outdoors at the time of the last frost. To get the best results, plant frost-resistant plants such as leeks, kale, and cabbage.

Another alternative is to plant fast-growing plants and then leave them on the ground for a brief amount of time. Leaf leaves can be picked in the first 30 days after the planting date, and therefore could be an excellent option. Kale requires approximately 65 days for maturation, however, the delicate young leaves are harvested in the early hours. Bush beans and peas are able to be harvested in just 6 weeks. The smaller beans should be harvested in the early stages to squeeze more fruit from your plant.

Hardiness Zone 3

Low Temperature: -30deg F to -40deg F.

A typical Growing Season is from four or five to six months.

Last Frost: Middle of May.

First Frost: Middle of September.

Information:

Zone 3 remains frigid, however the growing season lasts minimum an additional month or two the case of Zone 2. The ground begins to thaw early and stays frozen over a longer time in the summer months which means you can grow your produce during a longer time to grow.

What to Grow:

We're now entering the Hardiness Zones that offer plenty of options of zones to pick from when choosing the plants you want to cultivate. A longer growing time allows you to plant plants from Zone 4 or Zone 5 in the spring and summer seasons however don't count on these to survive the winter.

For vegetable varieties the root vegetables are suitable for zones 3. Greens with a leaf can thrive when planted in Zone 3. The following veggies can be cultivated in Zone 3

* Asparagus.

* Beans.

* Beets.

* Bell peppers.

* Broccoli.

* Brussels sprouts.

* Cabbage.

* Carrots.

* Cauliflower.

* Celery.

* Endive.

* Garlic.

* Leavey greens.

* Leeks.

* Okra.

* Onions.

* Parsnips.

* Peas.

* Potatoes.

* Pumpkins.

* Radishes.

* Rutabaga.

* Spinach.

* Swiss Chard.

* Tomatoes.

* Turnips.

* Zucchini.

It is also possible to cultivate certain fruits within the Zone. Some of the following fruit types can grow successfully in Zone 3.

* Some apple trees (Honeycrisp, crabapples, Sweet Sixteen, etc.).

* Blueberries.

* Bush Apricots.

* Cantaloupe.

* Currants.

* Pears.

* A majority of raspberries.

* Vibrant grapes.

* Watermelons.

Hardiness Zone 4

Low Temperature: -20deg F to -30deg F.

A typical Growing Season is Five months.

Last Frost: Middle of May.

First Frost: Middle of September.

Information:

We're now talking. Zone 4 is able to accommodate the majority of veggies and fruits, except some that are extremely sensitive to cold.

What to Grow:

The fruits and vegetables grown in Zone 3 are also planted in Zone 4. In addition, you are able to cultivate the following kinds of vegetables and fruits:

* The majority of apple trees.

* Most cherries.

* Corn.

* Cucumbers.

* Eggplant.

* The vast majority of wine grapes.

* Lettuce.

* Plums.

* Some strawberries.

It is possible to have hardy kiwifruit planted in this area throughout Zone 7. The regular kiwifruit isn't produced in this region.

Hardiness Zone 5

Low Temperature: -10deg F to -20deg F.

The typical growing season is five and a quarter months.

Last Frost: Beginning of May.

First Frost: Middle of October.

Information:

Zone 5 is considered to be one of the best zones to cultivate vegetables and fruits because there's hardly any fruits and vegetables you won't be able to grow during the 5 months of growing. It's possible that you won't be able of re-wintering certain plants, but you'll most likely be able to plant them every year.

What to Grow:

It is possible to grow all kinds of things in Zones 3 and 4. You can also grow the following vegetables and fruits:

* All apples.

* Blackberries.

* All cherry.

* All fruit.

* Peaches and nectarines.

Hardiness Zone 6

Low Temperature: 0deg F to -10deg F.

The typical growing season is six months.

Last Frost: Middle of April.

First Frost: Middle of October.

Information:

Zone 6 is a great area to plant the majority of vegetables and fruits, because it is located between the majority of crops' hardiness Zone zones. It is possible to grow overwinter many perennial plants and be able to grow the fall, spring and summer perennial crop.

What to Grow:

It is possible to grow a wide variety of fruits and veggies within Zone 6. The figs are the latest addition to the Zone 6.

Hardiness Zone 7

Low Temperature: 0deg F to 10deg F.

The typical growing season is six months.

Last Frost: Middle of April.

First Frost: Middle of October.

Information:

Zone 7 is a good zone to cultivate fruit and vegetables. Many perennials are able to be grown in this zone, and you are likely to get many varieties of annuals. The fall crops are quite common, and it is possible to cultivate winter crops during the mild winters.

Be aware of the summer temperature, because temperatures can begin to harm cool-weather plants. The best time to plant these crops is until the fall and spring months, and they may not flourish in the midst of summer's scorching heat.

What to Grow:

There are many varieties of fruit as well as vegetables within Zone 7. Certain apple varieties might not be suitable for Zone 7 or above. Kiwifruit is a recent arrival to the zone.

Hardiness Zone 8

Low Temperature: 10deg F to 20deg F.

The typical growing season is eight months.

Last Frost: Middle of March.

First Frost: Middle of November.

Information:

Zone 8 is a good place to farm through the entire season. Winter's coldest months could have snow that hinders agriculture as well as cold temperatures that can affect the crops that are sensitive to frost. The majority of perennials will survive winter months in Zone 8.

Introduce heat-sensitive plants in spring, or later in fall in cooler weather. You should wait until after the final frost to plant cold-sensitive crops.

Zone 8 can be quite dry, so you should take the dryness into account when choosing an area in which to grow plants. If you're in a situation of survival it is likely that you will require water either directly from the sky or an nearby source.

What to Grow:

There are plenty of fruit and veggies in Zone 8 so being attentive to how sensitive to heat plants are. Make sure you've got a reliable water source.

Hardiness Zone 9

Low Temperature: 20deg F to 30deg F.

The typical growing season is ten months.

Last Frost: Middle of February.

First Frost: Middle of December.

Information:

Zone 9 is usually grown all year round, so that you are cautious to plant frost-resistant plants in winter. There is a bit more humidity in Zone 9 and must be aware of the intense heat your plants can endure in the summer season.

The top of the range of the temperature certain plants are able to handle in the summer months in Zone 9.

What to Grow:

There are many varieties of fruit or vegetables that are zoned 9. Certain varieties of apricots may not be suitable for Zone 9 or above.

Hardiness Zone 10

Low Temperature: 30deg F to 40deg F.

Typical Growing Season: Year-round.

Last Frost: Middle of January.

First Frost: Middle of December.

Information:

Zone 10 can be cultivated throughout the year. Plant frost-tolerant plants during the later winter and early spring since there's some frosts. The plants that can be affected by heat must be planted earlier in the spring and in autumn since summers are typically hot in the Zone.

What to Grow:

Most fruit and vegetables in Zone 10. However, plants that are sensitive to heat will have a difficult time getting their crops to grow during summer.

The zone you're in is at the top of Hardiness Zone ratings for a variety of vegetables and fruits and therefore yields could be less than those you'd receive in previous zones. Being able to cultivate crops year-round is more than enough to make up any lower yields that you could experience.

Hardiness Zone 11

Low Temperature: Above 40deg F.

Typical Growing Season: Year-round.

Last Frost: None.

First Frost: None.

Information:

Zone 11 stays warm all of the year, and can be quite hot in summer. The frosts aren't too bad to be concerned over in Zone 11. However, there is a lot of heat to bear. A few areas of Zone 11 are inhospitable to plants, but there are other areas where you can plant vegetables, but must be aware of the heat.

What to Grow:

Be sure that your plants in Zone 11 are capable of enduring temperatures of up to 100 degrees. Make sure that any product you cultivate in this zone can withstand temperatures of 100 degrees F or more. Certain areas will be able plant food that flourishes in cooler climates throughout the autumn, spring and winter.

Heat Zones

Apart from the freezing temperatures that your plants will endure as well, you must know the amount of heat they'll suffer. Although you can use the Hardiness Zone map is a useful tool to determine the likelihood that your plants can be able to endure winter months, it does not offer a comprehensive image of the summer high temperatures that your plants are exposed to.

The map is a great tool to identify the Heat Zone you live in. The Heat Zones aren't in the same way as hardiness Zones and aren't listed as the Heat Zones on the websites selling seeds, or even on the majority of seeds' packets. There are a few seeds that are marked with this information however, you'll need to look for the Heat Zones.

Chapter 4: Sunlight And Shade

In reading the bulk of books on seeds, it is likely that you will find a few phrases that define the degree of sunlight or absence of sun, plants need sufficient sunlight to attain the point of maturity and to produce fruits. The plants require a certain amount of light each day to create food through photosynthesis. The amount of sunshine required by a plant differs from plant to.

When you've established how much sunlight your region will receive then you'll have an idea of the kind of plant to plant in the space. Certain species require complete sunlight while others require light shade while others need some combination of light and shade.

Below are the definitions for the most commonly used descriptors to describe the amount of sunshine the plant requires:

Full sunshine refers to the plant which requires at least six full hours of sunshine every day. The majority of full sun plants are able to take more than 6 hours of sunlight, however they may require additional water in order to prevent their skin from burning. The sun doesn't have to be constant. If the plant receives at least 6 hours throughout the day, it will be fine.

* Partially shaded or partial sunlight is the plant which requires between 3 and 6 hours of sunshine a day. The remainder of the day is best spent in shade from sunlight. Shade plants that are partial thrive in areas that are shaded by the scorching midday sun or the afternoon sun.

* Dappled sunshine is a phrase that's not often employed. It is a term used to describe sunlight which penetrates an overhead canopy, for example through the branches of a tree, or under an eaves-like canopy.

Full shade plants need less than three hours of daylight per day. Avoid thinking that plants in full shade can endure without sunshine. Plants require at minimum some sun to thrive. There aren't many veggies or fruits that ask for full shade.

It is possible to cultivate the plants you want in less optimal conditions, however these plants are usually restricted and have lower output than plants that are getting enough sunlight that they need.

Too Much or Too Little Sun

If you notice that your plants struggling due to the fact that they're receiving too much sun Try installing a shader near by to cast an overshadow on the plants during the most scorching time of the day. Offer struggling plants more irrigation to assist them.

These signs could indicate that the plant is being scorched from the sun's heat:

* Brown or burned leaf edges with browning towards the tips of stems.

Dry leaves, or flowers.

The colors of flowers or leaves may change.

The plant is either slowing or shrinking.

The area that's not getting sufficient sunlight could cause more problems than areas that receive overexposure to sunlight, as it's harder to fix. There are people who have set up reflectors in order to draw greater light to an area. However, it's difficult to control and isn't always effective. If you've got light that shifts throughout the day the container garden could be your ideal option. It is possible to grow your plants in containers that you move through the day so that the plants receive enough sunlight.

There are a few indicators that could suggest the plant isn't getting enough sun:

* The plant isn't developing as it should.

They are tiny and are scattered.

* The stems are brittle and incapable of supporting the weight of fruits or leaves.

* There aren't many flowers.

There is a limit to the yields of crop plants and any produce which does grow is tiny and stunted.

* The plant is trying to develop towards an illuminating source.

This is the perfect time to examine crops you're contemplating cultivating in an area that which you're not certain about. Incorrect assumptions about the area is a risk when you're relying on your yield to feed your family.

If you are considering the best place you'll plant your vegetables one of the other considerations you'll need to take into account is the length of your day. The sun's out much longer during the summer months as opposed to the winter's middle and so the plants that are planted during the summer months will get much more sunlight and an increased quantity of warmth. A region where you are in a position to grow cool weather plants in winter might not be ideal for the same crops in summertime.

Wind

People who live in areas that is prone to high winds may want to put up an enclosure or plant a hedge. You can also put up a windbreak to safeguard plants. The occasional ruffle of the wind from time from time to time could be beneficial as it can help plants grow more robust stems. The force of high winds, on contrary, could tear plants from the soil and deprive the plants of leaves and flowers.

In the event of strong winds could be pulled out of the ground when they do not have a strong root system. When you plant a survival garden the average wind speed as well as maximum wind speed should be weighed. If you reside in an area with strong winds, you should consider plant root vegetables or other varieties of plants that aren't likely to tear out of the soil.

It is important to note that a mild breeze could affect the cooling of plants as it will reduce the amount of water that is released by transpiration. However, a fast-moving wind during an extremely hot day could produce the opposite effect and dehydrate plants rapidly. If plants lose water too rapidly will shut their stomata and prevent the process of photosynthesis. The result is a slowing of growth, especially if this happens frequently.

The Environment

The surroundings are another aspect that needs to be considered while selecting seeds to plant. Take a look around the place where you intend to plant, and look for environment-related factors that might influence the plant's health.

Here are some of the various items that you must consider:

Do you have any structures in the vicinity? The structures of houses, homes as well as sheds and fences absorb heat, then release it, thereby raising temperatures of the air surrounding them. It can work for your benefit if you live in a cooler climate, and you want to plant plants that need warmer temperatures. This can hinder the gardening effort if you grow something that isn't able to handle all the heat radiating from the structure. They also offer shade at certain hours of the day. These may be detrimental or boon according to the plant that you're cultivating.

* Do you have some wooded areas in the vicinity? The wooded areas filled with trees and plants can cool the air around. Be aware of this when deciding what plants to plant. In addition, wooded areas are packed with creatures that can are able to sneak into your garden during the late at night to eat away at emerging crops.

Do you know of any lakes or bodies of water around? More expansive lakes and rivers can create unique weather patterns. For example, there could be wind or sleet, and sometimes snow blowing away from the water body. The problem with rivers is that they may flood during the spring as snow melts or when there are intense downpours that wipe out croplands around it. The areas around a big body of water tends to be warmer than the areas farther away from the body water.

Are there large stones in the vicinity? They can absorb an enormous quantity of heat, and emit warmth all day long. Similar to buildings that emit heat, rock can prove to be a problem or positive.

Make use of your surroundings to your advantage by thinking about what you'll plant as well as the location you'll need to place it.

Soil

Gardeners often overlook soil's role as a element when selecting the variety of seeds they want to grow. The soil is usually thought of as a standard, but actually, it can differ in terms of quality and character.

A healthy soil consists of many elements. The following substances are thought to exist in soil:

* Gases like air and others.

* Organic matter that is decomposing.

* Liquids.

* Microorganisms and living creatures.

* Minerals.

* Nutrients.

* Pollutants.

* Sand and rock.

* Water.

While it may appear to be similar, it's really made up of an array of different elements. It's available in various hues, textures and may have several specific characteristics that are unique to the region it's situated within. The kind and the quality of soil will affect the kind of plants you can effectively grow in a particular space.

Soil Layers

Soil is composed of five layers. They are also known as Horizons. From top to bottom they are as follows:

1. Horizon O.

2. Horizon A.

3. Horizon B.

4. Horizon C.

5. Horizon R.

Horizon O is the topsoil layer that you walk over. Horizon O is the layer of topsoil that you walk on "O" in Horizon O is "organic." The layer is usually less than one or two inches thick and is composed largely of organic matter which hasn't yet begun to degrade or is currently just beginning to decay. It's made up of microorganisms which reduce organic matter to the nutrients that are later made accessible to plants growing.

Horizon A follows and is a more dense stratum of the topsoil. Biomantle is also known as biosoil. it is composed of organic material complemented by minerals and it is the part of soil that has the highest amount of organic matter that has decayed and soil living things. Horizon A is where that earthworms, nematodes and centipedes along with fungi and an assortment of insects and microorganisms are accustomed to calling home. Horizon A is essential to the growth of plants since it is a major source of the essential nutrients needed by plants to thrive and grow.

Organic matter, in the form of compost or mulch could be added to soil's surface to enhance the organic appearance of soil. It will begin in Horizon O and will slowly descend to Horizon A as it decomposes and breaks down into smaller fragments. This can be a great option to provide organic material to an area where topsoil has disappeared due because of erosion.

Horizon B is referred to as the subsoil-level. It is composed of a mixture of substances including silicate clays, aluminum and iron. The layer tends to be more pale in hue and features distinct texture from the other layers. The roots of plants often get all the way to this layer however, there's not much to nourish them as they descend this far.

Horizon C is also known as the rock layer that is parent. The C horizon is usually composed of bigger pieces of rock that make the layers above it. When erosion and weathering take place it is possible for the C horizon to split and be an element of the horizons below it. The C horizon is usually composed of loose rocks that may be extracted using the help of a shovel when you go into the bottom.

Horizon R comprises large quantities of bedrock which aren't capable to be accessed by hand. It is typically found deep below the surface of Earth. The excavation must be 50 feet or more in certain areas to reach the bedrock.

Soil pH

Soil pH is an indicator of how acidic or alkaline the soil is. It's determined using an scale from zero to 14, where 0 is very acidic while 7 is neutral, and 14 indicating extremely alkaline. Some seeds are more tolerant of soils that are acidic and others like being slightly alkaline which is why it's essential to find out how pH-adjusted your soil.

The following are descriptive words used to describe the diverse pH ranges that soils can have:

Soil Type pH Range

Extremely acidic. Less than 4.5

Extremely acidic 4.5 to 5

Very acidic 5.1 to 5.5

moderately acidic 5.6 to 6.0

Very slightly acidic 6.1 to 6.5

Neutral 6.6 to 7.3

A little alkaline 7.4 to 7.8

Alkaline moderately 7.9 to 8.4

Very alkaline 8.5 to 9.0

Extremely alkaline Higher than 9.1

The pH of soil can be determined through a pH tester or test kits which are available from retailers which have a garden centre. If you want to get an accurate measurement you can try removing soil from your garden and send it for testing in a laboratory that is private or in a co-operative extension center.

The soil's pH determines the quantity of nutrients within the soil. The general rule is that slightly or moderately acidic soils are more nutrients available than soils that are alkaline however, soils that are strongly acidic could contain substances like aluminum which cause death to plants. The most diverse variety of nutrients is available for plants with a pH between 6 to 7.5.

The pH of the soil also affects the activities of microorganisms within the soil. The soil that is acidic has less microorganisms that are capable to break down organic matter.

It is possible for soil to become acidic with time because of the production of acids in decay of organic matter, and rainwater leaching the basic components away. To reduce the acidity of soil Lime can be added to the soil by way of wood or ash. If your soil is too alkaline to support the crops that you wish to cultivate organic mulch could be applied to the soil in order to raise the acidity. Sold soils that have a pH higher than 7.5 may be challenging to balance due there is a large quantity of calcium carbonate free within the soil.

Altering the pH of soil is not an easy job that requires many applications of the product that is used to alter the soil. Do not expect instant results. ensure that you take measurements in different parts of your yard, since the pH of soil can differ significantly from place to the location.

Soil Type

Three kinds of rock particles in soil.

* Clay.

* Sand.

* Silt.

The three rocks combine to create the different varieties of soil we're about to look at. They determine the appearance of the soil, its drainage capacity, and, to a lesser extent it defines the kinds of plants which can be established in the soil.

Clay soil is the least compact particle size of all three types of soil. It is sticky to the surface when wet, and it can hold a significant amount of water. Clay soil typically doesn't drain effectively and does not allow enough space for air to get through the clay. It's hard to work with when it is dry and is susceptible to causing damage when it is worked in a wet state. One advantage of clay soil is that it's able to store more nutrients as water does not drain straight through it to let the nutrients out.

Sandy soil contains the biggest particle size of all three. Larger particles permit the water to flow quickly across the soil. This means that the plants that are grown in sandy soil need greater amounts of water than in other soil types. Sand soil is simple to work with, however it is important to take extra care to ensure that the plants are getting the nutrition as well as the water they require.

Silt soil lies between clay and sandy soil with regard to its the size of its particles. It's surprisingly silky to the touch even if wet. Silt can hold water very well however, it is difficult to drain and is easily compacted. Be careful to make sure silt is well-aerated and isn't crushed.

The most suitable soil for gardeners is loam. It is a blend consisting of silt, sand and clay. Silt is very rich in Humus, an organic matter that has disintegrated into nutrients which can be absorbed by plants. Silt drains efficiently, it is well-aerated, and has plenty in organic matter.

To identify the kind of soil that you are using you need to add about a teaspoon of soil in the jar of glass and then fill it all up with water. Include a teaspoon of dishwashing detergent. Place the lid onto the jar, then shake it around. Let the jar rest on the counter for a night. The sand will fall down to the bottom. The silt will sit over the sand, and the clay will rise up to the highest point. The amount of each component will give you a clear idea of what kind of soil you've got.

Seed packets typically contain instructions that indicate what kind of soil that which a specific plant likes. If you try to plant seeds in different soil could result of frustration, therefore be sure to pay attention to the information.

Altitude

The higher the altitude, the air pressure declines, and the quantity of carbon dioxide in the air decreases. When you reach high altitudes, it is possible to discern where the carbon dioxide is too weak enough to sustain most plants by observing the timberline. At this point, when trees cease to grow, except for a handful of little stragglers that are stunted.

There are only a few plants are able to survive over the threshold of timber, therefore those who live above the timberline should find an area under the timberline in which they could grow their garden of survival. The timberline is found at various elevations across the globe.

There are a few crops that can grow at higher altitudes and this is contingent on the area and quality of the crop. The majority of coffee is harvested at heights that exceed five thousand feet. Grapes can be cultivated at elevations over 4,500 feet in certain regions around the globe.

Pollination may be a challenge when you are at higher elevations, as there might be a deficiency of flying insects when you've stepped outside their zone. Plants that are pollinated by wind can be a viable alternative, or you could be taught to manually pollinate the plants which you're cultivating. Winds that are strong can cause problems in higher elevations, and may hinder pollination.

Chapter 5: Putting It All Together

It's a bit overwhelming to consider in deciding on the best variety of seeds to suit the region you reside in. You must ensure that you select the correct plants for survival because they can become the one that makes the difference between life and becoming starving. In this case, the wrong choice could prove disastrous.

Here's an array of questions that you could ask yourself while selecting seeds for your seed vault. These questions will make sure you choose appropriate seeds. These questions can help determine the type of seeds that are best suited for the climate that you're planning on planting the seeds.

It is commonplace for people to enter the selection of seeds for making a cash-based survival plan by acquiring a wide variety of fruit and vegetables which they'd like to be able to cultivate. It's great if the seeds can be planted in the environment they'll be cultivated in. However, using the type of seeds that you'd like to use to use as your sole guideline for the seeds you'll gather could lead to a seed vault stuffed with useless seeds. This is particularly the case if you reside in colder climates or at high elevations, where several kinds of vegetables won't thrive.

Is This Seed Suited to the Hardiness Zone and Heat Zone I'm In?

The first thing to ask yourself when you're considering the possibility of planting a seed. There are times when you can grow vegetables from seeds not in the region that you're cultivating them however, you're putting yourself at an opportunity and should be aware of this at the outset. The result of a series of days which are too cool or too cold for the crop you're growing will have disastrous consequences for your crops.

An excellent general rule is that a large portion of the seeds that are in the vault that are suitable to your Heat and Hardiness Zone you are in, along with some other seeds to add. When you add seeds that you're not certain of to the vault, try them and find out if you are able to make them grow produce edible fruits or other vegetables. The watermelon seeds that are available around the globe aren't likely be a good idea in a region that's not ideal for the growth of watermelon.

Is This Seed Hybrid or GMO?

If so, you should not use the process. Hybrid seeds only develop exactly as they were in the first generation. You won't be able to gather seeds or cultivate future generations of the same species. GMO seeds have been genetically altered and pose a risk to the environment. Beware of both kinds and opt for the local heirloom varieties when they are available.

Do I Have an Area In Mind That Can Provide the Right Amount of Sunlight?

A lot of sun or many shade could ruin an entire plant. Be aware of the needs for sunlight of your plant before you add the seeds into your storage.

If you're in need of some shade but you do not have one, think about building a berm, fencing or any other kind or structure that can offer shade. It is possible to grow your plants next to an existing structure, close to trees, or even near the structure you have already built to offer shade in the heat in the heat of day. If you are in need of a sunny space, you might have the option of cutting down trees or move smaller structures, however the options aren't endless. Shade-loving plants may be planted around trees, allowing sunlight to be absorbed by their canopy, or it is possible to build latticework that will stop some sunlight.

Consider how many days of cloudy weather there are in your. There is a finite amount of sun when it is cloudy, and plants that need full sunlight might be stunted when you're experiencing a lot of cloudy days in the growth phase.

Will My Plants Be Subjected to Wind and/or Inclement Weather?

It is helpful to consider this issue from a worst case perspective.

What's the most dangerous kind of weather that you can endure and what is the strongest winds your crops are likely to be exposed to? If you think your crops won't be able to survive the worst case scenario, then it's time to look at other alternatives. If the most dire situation of weather or wind is observed during a situation of survival the chances are that you'll be in a famine and it's likely you'll get enough time to plant any more food or develop it in the time before starving.

It is possible that something as small like a berm or windbreak can make the difference between storms or inclement weather destroying the crop. Consider the best options and plan ahead and test your weatherbreaks before you have to utilize the breaks for survival.

Is This Plant Suited to the Soil It'll Be Planted In?

Take a look at the seeds' information attentively to determine if the information specifies what kind of soil that the plant likes. If you're purchasing your seeds via an online store Look for this info online. If you don't find it available on the website you're purchasing the seeds, do not feel intimidated to call or send an email to the seller. The seller may have the information, but they did not put it up on their website.

Choose the seeds that work best with your soil and the kind your soil is. You can also make your soil more fertile by incorporating enough compost or other organic materials into it, making it feasible. The soils of sandy and clay can be improved by the utilization of compost.

The pH of the soil is another importance. Be sure that the plants you're hoping to plant are able to thrive under the pH of your soil. possess.

Will This Seed Grow at My Current Altitude?

If you're living in the sea or are less than a thousand feet from sea level, then you don't need to be concerned about anything. A majority of seeds can be grown near sea level or just above sea levels. If you're at least a couple of hundred feet above sea level in the mountains or more it could be cause for significance.

Consider the height that you're located at as well as the impact that it will have on the plants. If you're over the trees, you'll experience difficulties growing most of the crop varieties. If you're located less than that line certain crops might grow while other crops will not. Make a decision today, to avoid doing the same thing when your life is at stake.

How Many Seeds Should You Save?

It is among the most frequent questions asked by those who have just begun the journey of survival seeds. The simple solution to this query is that you need to keep the seeds you can fit in and have the money for. There's no standard quantity of seeds to save, however, I'll tell you this. It is not advisable to end up with just 1 or 2 varieties of seeds during a crisis scenario. It's likely that you'll get exhausted of tomatoes even if it's the only one you've saved. Not to mention that in the end, you'll become being malnourished.

Variation is the key to success of life is full of it, and the greater varieties you can have and the more diverse you will be when the day is when you're required to count on your seed storage for food.

Heirloom seed packs are cheap, which means you can purchase a good selection of seeds at less than $100, and add them to your collection in the way you think appropriate. Seed packets cost around $1 per pack from $1 to upwards of $5 in a pack of 50-100 seeds. If you choose to stay on the low end of heirloom seed market, then you are likely to get between 5,000 and 7,000 seeds for each $100 you invest. It is recommended to collect at least one packet of each kind of plant you wish to grow, and then collecting several kinds of each.

I prefer to purchase my seed packets in different periods and from various suppliers which means I don't have to fret about a significant part of my supply going to waste in one go. I'd rather not purchase all my seeds from a single supplier, and then discover later that the seeds weren't good.

Start by obtaining seeds of local suppliers that have their crops close to the location you're in. This can help you ensure that you're purchasing seeds that work in your area. Make sure you purchase seeds that will thrive in the environment in which you're planning to start your garden for survival.

If you've accumulated a solid selection of local seeds It's time to expand to purchase seeds on the internet as well as from other trusted sources such as catalogs or the word of mouth. Look for seeds that are able to be planted in any growing season available. If you can it is your goal to have plants in the ground all year round. In the event that this is not possible due to of snow or frost choose plants that can withstand frost and allows you to prolong the growth time as much as is possible.

Once you've accumulated a substantial number of seeds that can be used locally within your garden, expand to purchase seeds that can be planted in other regions which have distinct conditions. There's no way to know the day you'll need to move from your home area and you'd prefer not to have to leave the seeds you have collected just to discover your seeds won't work in the new place you've relocated to.

It is recommended to purchase at least one packet of seeds to the region near you in every five packets you own that are suitable to your climate. The longer you stay the more areas that you've covered more well-prepared you'll become.

Are Survival Seed Vaults a Good Deal?

Personally, I'm not a fan of the survival seeds "vaults" or "banks" or whatever businesses that are promoting survival in the present. You can get an already-made collection of seeds that includes a variety of seeds. However, there are several problems with these vaults that make them unsuitable.

The biggest issue with purchasing seeds from a vault is that the seeds were hand-picked by another person. It's true that the person who chose the seeds might be a "expert" in the field of seeds for survival. Also, there's a possibility that the person wasn't an specialist. No matter the individual's degree of knowledge it's impossible for anyone could choose one set of seeds that will work for all situations available. Someone who lives within the Rocky Mountains is going to require a different selection of seeds compared to someone who lives close to deserts in Southern California. The person living located in Wisconsin will require specific seeds than a person living within Southern Texas.

It's not logical to create a collection of seeds and claim to provide survival it's unlikely to benefit many individuals who are buying it when they require it the most.

If you reside in an area with a mild climate, in which almost anything could develop, your survival seed vault could contain seeds that which you could utilize. However, you may think about purchasing seeds for yourself in order to save money. The survival vaults are generally pricey because they make money from the fear of being stranded without food. I've come across Survival seed vaults that are outrageously priced for the amount they offer. Although there aren't all seed vaults that are counterfeit, there are plenty in the sense that I suggest to at the very least price what the cost would be to purchase the seeds separately.

Another issue I face with seed vaults is the ambiguity of nature and provenance that the seeds come from. They may proven to be from an reputable source however, there's a possibility that they aren't. I would rather purchase my seeds from trusted suppliers who have a long-standing reputation in the business of selling high-quality seeds. In the meantime, I'll test the seeds in a couple of packets the seeds I purchase for confirmation that they are of excellent germination rates.

How Much Produce Will You Need?

In order to produce enough food enough to satisfy the needs of a single person it will require around 4,000 square feet of cultivable space. In order to meet the demands of four members of a family it will require approximately 16,000 sq feet cultivable space. It's a lot of land that can be used by one person of 63'x 3'. If there's not this type of land available however, you might be able to prolong the harvest of your land by planting several varieties in a series.

If we assume that every person in your household will require around 2,000 calories per every day for their survival. If you're in a small space then you'll prefer growing nutritiousas well as calorie-dense veggies to maximize the number of amount of calories that you can produce per square feet. The legumes, the corn and potatoes are all food items that provide a lot of calories. The three vegetables kale, lettuce and spinach are all high in nutrients that are great for an organic garden.

It's more beneficial to underestimate your requirements than underestimating your needs. Additional fruits and vegetables are able to be canned and kept for winter. These guidelines are general guidelines that will guide you to the correct ballpark.

You are free to alter the settings to meet your requirements.

Crop Amount to Plant Per Person

Asparagus up to 10 sq. feet

Avocados 1 tree per person

Beets range from 10 or 15 square feet

Broccoli Three to five plants

Brussels grows 3 to 5 plants

Bush beans can cover 8-10 square feet

Pole beans ranging from 8 to 10 square feet

Plants of Cabbage 5 to 7

Carrots, 10 square feet

Plants of Cauliflower 3 to 5.

3 to 5 plants of Chard

Corn 10 sq. feet

Cucumbers up to two mounds

Plants of Kale to 3 or 5

The leafy greens can cover up to 20 square feet

Onions from 6 to 8 sq. feet

Peas ranging from 8 to 10 square feet

Radishes up to 15 sq. feet

Sweet peppers that range from 10 to 15 sq. feet

2. Squash 2 to 4 mounds

A tomato with 5 to 8 vines

Turnips ranging from 8 to 10 square feet

The Watermelon 1 to 2 vines

How to Store Survival Seeds

Seeds begin to germinate when the climate is appropriate and the oxygen and water are available in sufficient quantities. For the proper storage of seeds, it is essential to ensure that they don't get to the proper temperature, and aren't able to get an access point to the liquid or oxygen they require to germination. Also, you should protect them from the direct sunlight.

If you can keep these three elements out of the way and from being able to reaching your seeds, you'll be in a position to preserve seeds for a lengthy amount of time before they are required to be replaced. The seeds of some varieties can be stored for between 10 and 20 years, or even longer depending on the seeds kind, the degree to which they've been dried, as well as the efficacy of the storage method.

Dry Your Seeds First

If you have collected the seeds by yourself you must ensure they are dried to the point that they contain between 4% and 8% water. The most efficient method to dry the seeds is to bring them to temperatures of 100 degrees F and leave the temperature for between 6 and eight hours. If you're purchasing seeds from a reliable supplier, they'll already have dried, and you may do this without a problem.

These methods can be utilized for drying seeds:

Set the food dehydrator at 100 degrees F and then dry the seeds for six hours.

• Place the seeds into an oven that is gas-powered and then use your flame to dry the seeds. Place the seeds inside the oven for six hours.

Make use of the inside lighting of the electric oven to warm seeds to a temperature of 100 degrees F in 6 hours.

The conventional oven should be turned at its lowest setting. Then make sure the door is open so that the heat inside the oven is at 100deg F. Dry the seeds for six hours.

* Spread the seeds on a sheet and then dry in the sunshine. It's more difficult to reach 100 degrees F by this method, so you'll need to monitor the seeds with a keen eye and take away from the sun once they've dried.

If you believe they aren't be sure to check them thoroughly before you store them. Bend the larger seeds into half. The seeds should break before you're in a position to connect one end one to the opposite. You can hit larger seeds using the Hammer. They will break up and fall into dust.

Blocking light, oxygen and water from reaching the seeds

Your method of seed storage is only as effective as the container in which the seeds are placed in. If your container lets air and oxygen to enter the storage process, it is inadequate and shelf life of your seeds could be dramatically diminished. It could be risky since seeds don't show signs degrading. When seeds are damaged, they will not germinate on the ground.

To prevent moisture and air from getting into your seeds, they must to be kept inside an airtight container. For a quick check to determine whether a container truly airtight, you need to seal it. Then set it inside a bowl of water. Then, weigh it until it's completely submerged, and then leave it for at least a few days. If you see water in the container after you take it from the tub, then you'll be aware that it's not a suitable container for storing your seeds.

Do not assume that the packets that seeds arrive in are airtight. It is possible to keep them inside the containers to provide an additional layer of security, but they should not be the sole factor that separates seeds from the world outside. A few people put the seed packets inside airtight Tupperware containers. Other people prefer freezer bags that are sealable. The container is wrapped in an airtight bag, to keep any light from contacting the seeds.

Another alternative is to pack them in a vacuum seeds. This can prolong the life of the seeds since vacuum packing removes a lot of humidity and air inside the container, and stops new humidity and air from forming their way into. However, it is recommended to keep the seed pack vacuum enclosed in a plastic bag to prevent light from entering.

There's an easy trick you can apply to safeguard your seeds from water. The seeds should be placed in the airtight bag or container and then seal the bag. The sealed bag should be placed in an additional container with a sealable lid. Include rice, dry milk or a desiccant packet or two into the outside container, and then seal it. The moisture now needs to make it through several layers of security prior to getting into the container.

Label the containers as you are packing the seeds. There's no reason to open a lot of boxes when looking for a specific type of plant, especially if there is a huge collection. It is important to put the date on the packaging in order discern which seeds were put in the package. away.

Chapter 6: Keep Seeds Cool

The seeds that are kept at room temperature are slowly, but steadily less and less robust until they're ineffective. The embryonic stage of the seed is consuming the energy units in the seeds while waiting for sun, water and oxygen which will never arrive.

If a seed is left to grow at room temperature to die slowly while the embryo is slowly, but gradually, depleted of nutrients.

The process of putting seeds in the freezer puts them into a state of suspended animation. This means that they're healthy enough to come back to life and begin germinating when returned to normal temperatures, however they will not draw up a large amount of store-up energy. The seeds could be stored in cold basement, storage space, or even in the fridge.

The seeds should be left at temperatures at room temperature for a week or two prior to trying to start to germinate.

Testing the Germination Rate

If you're unsure whether seeds are viable that you've stored for some time check the germination rates of the seeds periodically to confirm that they're functional. Even when they're stored in ideal conditions, seeds could be rotten and you don't wish to spend a lot of time and energy making seeds from which only a little (or any at all) can develop into plants that are viable. It's a high risk when you're gardening to survive, which is why it's essential to shift your odds as far in your favor as is possible.

As the seeds age in the soil, they do not all go to death in one go. They will gradually die, there are a few here, and there until the rate of germination has dropped to zero. Whatever method you choose to store them in the longer you put off to grow seeds, the higher likelihood they'll be destroyed and the less seeds that will be feasible.

To determine if the seeds are germinating, spread fifteen to twenty seeds between two moist paper towels. Set them in an area with temperatures that range between 65deg F between 75 and 65deg F and then let them rest until they sprout. Monitor the seeds on a regular basis and observe if they are germinating. Certain seeds such as corn, wheat and legumes could require soaks in water prior to beginning to grow. Certain seeds might also require stratification meaning that they'll need be exposed to temperatures below freezing for a specific duration before they can develop.

If the rate of germination is lower than around 70%, then it's time to look at the replacement of your cache or making it a new one and collecting seeds from the area. It's an excellent idea to establish an area of survival where it is possible to gather both seeds, and grow well ahead of having depend on your abilities for survival. Seeding your garden to harvest new seeds as well as change your seed stock can be a fantastic method to get started.

Organic Soil Amendments

Soil amendments include organic composts, fertilizers made from natural materials, and manure, which are incorporated into soil to make sure it has all the essential nutrients that plants require for growth. It is also possible to add them gradually to alter the pH of soil you are growing in so that it is more suitable for the plants that you would like to plant.

You shouldn't be able to depend on amendments for soil which you purchase from a shop because the store might not be operational during emergencies that last for long. If they're operating, the probability that they have soil amendments on hand at an affordable price is very unlikely.

A few soil amendments are suitable for stockpiling however, your stock is likely to run out. If this occurs then you'll need access to all the organic ingredients available. We'll look at some of the numerous organic ingredients that could be added to your soil.

Compost

Compost is about as close as it can be to an all-inclusive soil amendment. It's made up of various organic matter that's decomposed.

It's abundant in nutrients, and has the potential in order to boost the organic matter of all soil types. Compost is a clear source of the humus that plants require to be large and robust.

The great thing about compost is that it can be made it in your home. The compost is made using an old wooden container or a tumbler that is specifically designed for it or wire crate, or any other container that you are able to dump organic matter into, and then let it decay.

Chapter 7: The Complete Guide To Growing And Storing Vegetables, Fruits, Herbs

AND FLOWERS SEEDS

Everyone includes vegetables as a part of their daily diet. We are advised that we have a daily intake of fresh vegetables. It's fun to plant and cook vegetables for yourself. The question is what kind of vegetables to grow. There will be guidelines and ideas regarding how to grow vegetables.

If you're looking for ways to plant veggies in your backyard It's really not difficult. Producing vegetables needs lots of sunlight. This is why you must check if your garden has enough sun. Beginning in spring and establishing a vegetables in the vicinity of your kitchen will always be the best. So it is easy to get access to the garden that will allow for faster plant. Seeds must be moist and will require humidity. They're ready to germinate when they're big. Most vegetables such as cabbage and broccoli do not require the seeds to be soaked. If you overdo it, the process of soaking can damage seeds. Be careful not to throw them away in a hurry.

In the event of deciding the best way to plant vegetables that are cold-hardy conditions, you'll require Tepees which are packed with water around soft veggies. Other plastic sheets are accessible on the market which provide a barrier the plant once it's fully filled with water. Additionally, sun rays will easily travel across the sheet, ensuring that plants are warmer for a longer time. It is recommended to plant these plants deep within the earth.

Are you wondering what you can do to cultivate vegetables that are grown on vines. If you place the vines in your backyard it is possible that they will not develop according to the way you'd like them to, and may expand into the yard. If they're rooted deeper, they are able to be maintained easily. They require horizontal plantation within the trench. The seed does not require a deep sown into the soil. It is able to grow.

Beware of cutworms, which can harm delicate and tender plants. This will help you save space when gardening with vegetables if ensure that you position the plants vertically. It's possible to permit fruits and vegetables like cucumbers melons, beans etc. to grow in the walls or trees, instead of being spread all around the area. The two vegetables require regular fertilizers. Be sure to take proper treatment of these. They will provide vegetables on frequent times.

It can go far more smooth than you'd think. There are other aspects that go into the cultivation of plants in your garden gardens that you might have not previously considered. It can turn out to be rewarding and enjoyable when you understand the primary factors.

These are the secrets to obtaining good plants. Every plant has what it requires. In the same way it is important to shield our plants from items they do not need. This is why division essential to the success of a plant. Locate one of the primary plants' needs that is water. Some plants may need significantly greater amounts of water than others. The gardens in your home are supplied with the water by either rainfall or directly watering. It is best to plant plants that have similar water needs close. In this way, when the water is used it is less of a concern which direction the water goes. Landscape design is more crucial in case of rain. It is recommended that plants with little water be placed in a soil that is suitable so that they can drain, and there are instances when plants that require more water must be handled with the effective soil selection as well as various other methods. The requirements for planting include a lot of what you can do to plant vegetables, however there's a different aspect of the garden that shouldn't be ignored.

Plants do not have a singular mind. Plants have the capacity to interactions. Maybe you've heard about the tale of crossing of pollinated plants. Perhaps you have also encountered people who mixed flavors into plant species that were growing close to one another. The second reason is for separating correctly. There's a wide variety of pollinating plants all over. If you want to let the plants to develop and develop in the natural process, examine the plants you'd like. There are times when you could choose to plant neutral plants to separate the interconnected plants. There are times when you might be required to remove an empty space within your garden. But, generally it is possible to plant something you can plant on the spot that is empty.

If you take this into consideration in mind, you'll be able to have a good, and simple knowledge of what you can do to plant vegetables in your vegetable garden. This doesn't mean that your garden should stay the same year after year. There are a couple of areas in many gardens that change each year. This gives variety to vegetable garden, but in certain situations, they can improve the soil quality in the gardens. It is possible to combine them in a variety of ways that will add more enjoyment in your gardening. This also means that you'll need to share even more amazing veggies with your friends. Smiles are bound to continue invigorating those who consume the veggies to get involved in gardening. It is possible that they are not fond of the task, but many be enthralled by watering and other actions.

The process of growing vegetables can be fun. It is a long process in preparing the soil before you plant the seeds, however it's well worth it to have the option of choosing the freshest cucumber or tomato as a side dish. A lower grocery cost when you can is an advantage. Although it's not difficult to grow, vegetables requires some knowledge.

The vegetables can be grown by two methods. It is possible to grow them in an outdoor greenhouse that is typical and you could also plant the vegetables in pots. Whatever method of gardening you decide to take an area that is sunny is the only constant for each. If trees are within your backyard pruning them will increase the amount sunshine your garden gets. It is possible to move them around and enjoy sunlight for long durations of time, based on the weight and size of containers.

Learning how to plant the vegetable garden in order to reap the maximum amount of satisfaction

Container gardening is a great way of gardening vegetables even if you don't have enough space on the property. The majority of vegetables that are produced in container gardens are tomatoes, eggplants or peppers as well as squash. Certain vegetables require the minimum of one gallon and others require more. Containers that are compost-filled are the best made for gardening in containers. The seeds of vegetables can be planted as early as. The seeds should be planted in a sunny spot in order to be prepared for transplanting once the season gets underway. Plants for starting can be bought from the local garden center.

It is possible to plant within your backyard a classic vegetable garden. Pick a spot where sunlight is abundant for the majority of the time. Take a look at the space that your garden can cover and then calculate the area. There are two main reasons it is essential to measure the space. First, it is to determine what amount of fertilizer or mulch could be needed and secondly for deciding the number of plants that can be planted.

After the soil is fertilized and prepared in accordance with the instruction follow the instructions to plant seeds or start-up plants.

The overcrowding of your garden can't allow your plants flourish which means you'll have very little or no vegetables. The crop you choose to plant the germination process can last anywhere from one week to six weeks, regardless of where the seeds are planted. If you plant starter plants the plants will need several days for them to mature and look dead. It is important to water the plant or seeds after the planting. The soil must be moist, but not saturated.

Containers need holes in the bottom, to let water drain and should be set upon blocks or bricks. They must be positioned in lawns that are graded to ensure that the water doesn't get buried. In the event of rain, it isn't necessary to water. Don't water with a torrent of water, but by an easy sprinkle.

You can set sprinklers in your landscape on a rainy day for just a couple of minutes.

KEEPING THE GARDEN FREE FROM RABBITS

T

That is why you should regularly weed. If weeds allow themselves to grow in your garden, they'll take the energy of the soil, leaving the plants without much or none of the energy. The garden might require fencing or a protection from animals.

The best way to plant a vegetable garden requires you be aware of what plants require in order to flourish. Therefore, do not be worried about the new plant you've chosen to grow and I'll guide you through the entire process. We will go through the essentials necessary to prepare your garden in order.

• Clear the fields Make sure the area is suitable for your crops. What can you do to determine if you're in the right place? Make sure to sweep it up cleanly so that there are no weeds or leaves which could be a hindrance to your garden's growth.

The first step is to have to till the soil thoroughly and disintegrate it to ensure your garden will breathe.

Once the soil is tilled, and removed The fertilizer you want to add is put in.

When the fertilizer has been sprayed then you must make sure to till again the soil in order so that the fertilizer is blended in order to allow it to work at its full potential.

Then, you apply a bit of water on the soil. Do not apply a large amount of water. Make sure that no remains in the soil's edge.

The process of growing the vegetable garden is going to take a lot of experimentation and trial So don't worry when you fail initially. If you're adding excess water, simply wait a few days, and then try it to do it again.

It is now ready to plant after you have applied the water and the soil has become damp and has no settled

Look at how simple this was. The first vegetable garden is clear and is now waiting to be planted. The fun is getting started. It's time to get your seeds of choice from your local nursery.

Melons and cucumbers are easy to cultivate within compost. Food scraps and leftovers are used to fertilize them. This will act as manure and help the plant to flourish. It's the best method for growing these veggies.

There's a wide variety of veggies you could easily cultivate in your garden. After you've laid out the space and decided on what you want to plant, is the time to plant the plot with plants and get them to expand. It's not enough to just put vegetable seeds in the garden and then wait for they to grow and produce new food. There are many varieties of vegetables that thrive under different circumstances and require different nutrition over other varieties. Here are some helpful ideas from only a few well-known varieties that you can get the most benefit out of.

Peas

It's a wonderful sound to hear a delicious large pea pod opening to reveal the first peas in the season can be a pleasant experience. Peas for me are a sweet treat for the world. It's an amazing thing that someone returns in my home kitchen! It is important to dig your soil thoroughly when you plant peas and add lots of manure prior to planting as peas are fond of moist soil. The mulching around the base of each plant as well as frequent watering can aid them during droughts that they dislike. In the end, sowing outside will be contingent on your area however, it is usually from mid-spring to early spring. First, make sure that your soil is warm enough. Peas must be secured with stakes or sticks that allow plenty of spaces on the plants to allow pods to develop. Peas are popular among birds and so covering plants that are young with chicken wire or nets is a great option. The pods are harvested regularly to make sure they're fresh and ready to make use of or freeze them as required.

Runner beans

I recommend people who have no experience in growing vegetables growing runners beans. They are quick to grow and require minimal effort. They are stunning and come with a the longest harvest times and produce a large harvest. There are just three primary conditions for runner beans. They are well-drained soil, plenty of well rotted manure, and plenty of water. There is a need for a solid infrastructure to grow the runner beans. Obelisks of high bamboo, or solid sticks are the best climbing structures. It is important to place your stakes up the early hours and ensure they are well protected The weight they will become once they're filled with beans is amazing! Plant the seeds indoors from between mid-spring to early spring. The new plants are then transplanted in spring at the base of an supported structure that is upright. As they approach the high point of the support structure, pull the upward tips to ensure that they don't become top heavy. Pick the pods at a time when they're still young, and could be stiff until they begin to expand as older pods.

Tomatoes

The sweet and tangy taste of fresh tomatoes right off the vine is very enjoyable. They can be grown in your greenhouse, the growbag, or even in your garden. They are best grown in the greenhouse since it is more likely to produce a higher quality crop since the plants are not too dependent on their environment. Avoid growing seeds tomatoes. They can be complicated, and you'll have more than you could make use of or sell. Gardener's joy is a beloved among mine. This cultivar produces an abundance of sweet and delicious small cherry tomatoes. You can pinch the growth tip of plants after five or six fruit-bearing side shoots that look healthy are developed. Feed your tomatoes. They'll be grateful to all summer long.

Potatoes

Potatoes, according to vegetable gardeners, are a very easy plant to cultivate that is used to ensure an abundant harvest. If you don't have enough space for maincrop as well as early varieties, I would advise you to focus on early varieties of salad. Nothing is more enjoyable than digging out the early salad potatoes of summer and having them cooked with a good butter drizzle. Potatoes for seed need to be chit-chit before planting; this means that they're sprinkling short green shoots. Planting potatoes should begin as early as the middle of spring. The best way to construct trenches is by surrounding the potato. Take each potato with care in order to make sure that the shoots don't get removed. The potato should be planted to 15cm, and having a gap of 30 centimeters between the potatoes. If the sprouts rise from the soil, begin the earthing-up process by spreading the soil and on top of them to form an incline. This stops the tuber from becoming exposed to light, and turning dark green. This makes they harmful. It is important to water young plants regularly to ensure that the tuber is well-cultivated. Keep an eye out for the potato blight, which in the summer months that are hot and humid, could be an issue that may ruin your crop. The first time you harvest potatoes, it's as if you are searching for treasure. After the plants have bloomed it is time to harvest. Pick a dry, moist day, and rub a little of soil off to determine whether the tubers are big enough. Let the tubers be open to air and let them dry for several hours. It makes it easier to handle.

Carrots

Have you ever wondered why people take the time to cultivate carrots, when they're affordable to purchase and can be stored effectively? But I doubt you've tasted any carrot until you've eaten ones you've grown your own. Its flavor is richer and more sweet. The carrots can be planted regularly during the months of March through July however, don't begin too early because the soil must be very warm in order to allow effective germination. Carrots are one of the vegetables which does not enjoy transplanting and should be planted directly in the soil. Carrots require a smooth healthy, well-drained soil without obstructions in order to prevent twisted or club roots. So, planting them in a large gardens with a free-draining seal compost or soil can be much more efficient. The carrot seed should be planted thinly however it can be difficult because the seeds are small and the seeds are likely to shrink once they begin to emerge. Avoid flying carrots during the early the summer. You should consider growing chives near your carrots as aroma of the chives can be good enough to cover the scent of carrots that attracted the flies. The carrots should be kept out in the fields till the end of time. Once they are harvested, the better these are the more delicious the taste!

Chapter 8: How To Grow Vegetables In Winter

Most people believe that the season for growing vegetables ends with the month of September. It begins the month of April or in May. While this may be one of the seasons that you enjoy the most pleasant temperatures and the chance to enjoy more outdoor time - winter is not considered to be a "dead season."

Alongside getting your soil prepared for the approaching spring, you could be practicing winter planting as well as well as continue growing your crops. In this article, I'll discuss two main issues in this piece by using seasonal extenders to lengthen seasonally "warmer" season and growing vegetables in the winter months to be harvested in the spring.

What is the reason I continue to grow plants after they become cold?

In winter You can make use of"so-called "season extenders" to retain some warmth to the plants as well as protect your plants from snow and wind harm. These include:

Create small row covers big enough to be able to cover your plant life; or you could create a type of greenhouse that you could use to work and enter.

Furthermore, the advantages of these systems is that they utilize the greenhouse effect in order to heat the air beneath the covers. But, when it is cold during the winter it is the case that cold-resistant plants grow most effectively.

If you utilize greenhouse vegetable plan of planting, you can be planted at almost any time of the all year. In a hothouse, growing vegetables is similar to cultivating vegetable gardens in summer. It is just a matter of taking some extra steps to create artificially the conditions you would get under normal circumstances.

Two methods can be used to cultivate the plants in an outdoor greenhouse that is portable. In the course of the day, one utilizes the heat from the sun to generate heat for the system and is known as the cold method. If the temperature decreases then a heating device turns on, ensuring that the temperature stays to at least 45 ° F. It is not the case that plants thrive with this method and are instead kept in check until they are moved outdoors in summer.

The growing of vegetables during winter requires water. The best method to choose is using a warm method. Greenhouses for garden use must maintain an ideal temperature of 55 ° F in order to grow and need the use of a heater. Heating equipment can include natural, propane or electrical.

In a greenhouse, almost every vegetable grows outside is able to be grown indoors. Each vegetable comes with an indoor variety that are cross-bred. In the majority of catalogs they will have seeds that are able to be planted in winter. The seeds you are looking for are ones that do not require much heating to grow. It is important to look for varieties that are compact or able to be trimmed down in size as in the systems mentioned, there's little space for a garden.

Pollination is an important nature-based process that must be artificially induced. In reality, insects cannot reside within the plant, especially insects, particularly bees. The process of pollinating tomatoes can be a good example of pollinating vegetables. The tomato vines must be affixed to bamboo stakes The stakes must be struck in the early morning and at night after the bloom is finished. When the petals begin curving inwards then the flower has finished. Be aware of this because the flower may contain pollen for only three days in order to pollinate the crop.

Because there's not much sunlight during winter, you must make use of sunshine with heating lamps. The majority of vegetables require an average of 8 hours of sunshine per day. Plants will have to be fed and watered.

It is more laborious and can take longer than the summer season, however it's also a lot of fun. If it is a cold day in January, visit the greenhouse to choose a tomato which has been ripe by the vine. Whatever time it is it is possible to enjoy all the flavors of summer.

There are a variety of season planting plants which can be planted at the end of winter and fall months (also in the winter months when the fields are frozen). Actually, certain species (so-called cold-season crops) are designed to be planted earlier than later in the year, will not develop as fast.

The advantage of planting earlier is the fact that it allows for a.) you will get high-quality, robust plants, and

b.) that you can harvest your crops more quickly (in the spring rather than during summer).

It is also important to remove your bed of dead plant matter (also leaves from the autumn) prior to planting seeds. Break the soil open, then apply the compost until it is incorporated. Organic fertilizers are a good option in the event that your soil has been heavily cultivated in the past year.

Common cold and hardy plants look like this:

The tubers and the roots shouldn't be planted at the beginning of the year as they are susceptible to rotting due to the moisture. However, if you mix these two suggestions, cold covers and plants that are cold seasonally, you could even plant potatoes earlier than they're due. Then, you can move them to the "natural" beds once the temperature warms up.

I hope this will motivate you to grow your own garden in winter.

AQUAPONICS-HOW TO GROW VEGETABLES QUICKLY

Aquaponics - How to Create and Operate a Setup

This is perhaps the most crucial issue that came up as we considered growing fish and veggies in tandem. It is the practice of growing plants and fish with the smallest amount of resources - mostly the water that is already in the fish tank. The idea of making use of waste material generated by your fish ponds is to provide your plants with nutrient-rich soil.

It's surprisingly simple and an entirely organic method to plant your most loved vegetables, without having to think about the cultivation of soil or fertilization in addition to the harmful chemical fertilizers. All you have to do is feed your fish with an aquaponics system or you could even grow the fish's food yourself.

Aquaponics: How do you utilize the latest fish tank?

Before we dive into Aquaponics details, let's look at how the water in your tank of fish is beneficial in the cultivation of plants. We are all aware that fish create a great deal of waste. It also produces ammonia. This, when allowed to accumulate, can be harmful to fish (a important reason for why you should refresh your water in an ordinary system at intervals, without a proper filtering system installed). Plants are the ones that filter water in an aquaponics plant. They, however, are not able to employ ammonia. The reason is that the bacteria that live in tank water can grow naturally and will transform the ammonia into Nitrates. These nitrates function as a natural fertilizer to any kind of vegetable, which gives you the unique chance to cultivate fresh produce by using the natural waste of fish.

The results of research have proven that growing vegetables using the water of fish tanks can cause the plants to expand at a rate of fifty percent faster than normal. Additionally, you have the opportunity to observe your favourite vegetables develop quickly. But that's not all. The same water could be recycled to the tank that has been filtered which will help keep the fish within a clean living environment.

Aquaponics: How to begin:

The fundamental process to begin in Aquaponics is easy. In order for plants to thrive it is necessary to have fish ponds as well as reservoirs. Kits that are already built are available in the marketplace, but the system you choose to build can easily be developed and built. What ever you choose to build what you do, the only thing you should be aware of to get going with aquaponics is

1. What do you want to cultivate?

2. Living room available,

3. This is the kind of system you'd like to build.

After it is established, aquaponics won't need a lot of time to take care of. Fish tanks remain below the level of those that rise, regardless of the method you decide to employ, as the water that flows from the beds will flow back into the tank. Keep in mind that the water will be reused and this is the reason why aquaponics can only consume about 2 percent of water employed in your backyard gardening.

The pump is needed that can bring in a specific quantity of water to the beds to ensure that the plants get the right quantity of water that contains the essential nutrients and then transfer it back to the tank, where it is filtered. There are certain procedures that require plants' roots are immersed within the mud. the mud drains into the plant.

Aquaponics benefits you for three reasons: you obtain fresh veggies, you obtain fresh fish, and you'll save some money.

Aquaponics is especially suited for regions with a very limited access to water, since it only requires a small amount of water. It can help provide much-needed nutrition is a great idea for countries that are in the third world. It's also extremely beneficial to understand how to establish an aquaponics plant as it provides us affordable fresh vegetables as well as fresh fish. In particular, when the cost of fresh vegetables is sky-high due to the weather.

How to Raise Year-round Vegetables With Indoor Aquaponics

With aquaponics, you can build an indoor garden you won't have to contemplate spending the outrageous winter prices for fresh produce. Or, in the room in the basement or a spare bedroom, you could grow plants all year round. Find something fresh! Perhaps the most exciting thing to consider is you will have first-hand information about what you're eating.

If you're not familiar with aquaponics, I'll swiftly get you up level. Aquaponics is in essence the extension of hydroponics. It is the practice of growing plants without using soil or dirt. Plant roots rest directly on a bath of water. It is generally believed that the plant's roots are in an unsteady bed. Hydroponics is a method of feeding the plants, it was necessary to supplement the nutrients in the water.

The plants can get their nutrition in a more organic and sustainable manner through aquaponics. This is due to the raising of fish. If you've had fish in the past, you're aware that they release unpleasant byproducts, like ammonia and the like. Here's the place how we experience the wonderful circle of life. These unpleasant by-products are the things plants require to thrive. So, the fish emulsion provides food for plants as well as they purify their water to benefit the fish while the plants absorb all they require out of the water. It is a natural, and completely organic procedure.

If you're thinking about what type of plants can be grown by aquaponics it's a lot happening. For beginners, it is recommended to start with a leafy vegetable such as lettuce. The fastest growth rate is typically for lettuce. Some plants that you could add are watercress, basil, tomatoes, peas, tomatoes, green and red peppers melons and strawberries as you become comfortable with the process. There are many options to try. A true indicator of whether the plant is beneficial to your needs or not is to experiment and try it out.

Another benefit of aquaponics is that it can be beneficial to the environment. It allows you to consume the fish too! If you're seeking an option to be eco-friendly (or free of the grid) This kind of garden will not only provide fresh fruit and other vegetables all year long as well as proteins. It can be done from the convenience in your home.

Most likely, you think it will be costly to invest in an indoor system for growing aquaponic plants you think? It's true, especially in the event that you buy an already-built device, it could be true. It's good to know it is completely possible to create your own device using an excellent DIY tutorial. The savings on your bills for commodities will be enough to cover operating costs. In addition, you will have the benefit of knowing which food items in your family is sourced from and if it's secure.

Chapter 9: How To Grow Vegetables In Containers

The benefits of growing plants in containers have many benefits. The soil will be maintained better. Additionally, there are more options when it comes to dealing with fluctuations in temperature and light. Controlling insects is thus simpler. In a residence in the backyard, or inside a greenhouse, garden containers can be cultivated.

Certain vegetables take up huge amounts of space for example, pumpkins and cucumbers. However, they will perform well in pots. The peppers, peas and carrots and tomatoes all do equally well in containers or even more so.

It is crucial to choose the right container that can accommodate an established, fully-grown and harvest-ready plant. Pick soil that is clean of weeds, and make sure you have plenty of fertilizer prior to plant. Take a look at the synthetic soil such as peat moss, mixtures of or wood chips. You can also use perlite to suit the species you want.

Make sure you make sure to prepare your soil, or you can use an artificial medium prior to the planting. This will make controlling the water a lot easier. In order to keep plants in the containers in good health, it's essential to ensure adequate drainage as well as proper retention of moisture. Put some marbles in the lower part of the container to prevent the blockage of drainage holes. This will also ensure good drainage. Blend the clay into the industrial soil that is ready to be planted.

Additionally, if soil preparation is good be sure to water the soil cautiously. If the containers are near windows, soil could get dry quickly. When you overwater, it's simple to create root rot, or forget the watering tasks have been accomplished, so be sure to ensure you have a soil moisture test near.

Most of the time purchasing well-proportioned container planting soil will be less difficult. The soil that is poured from outside generally is not a suitable selection for the development of a container. Nature provides a method to get rid of water in clay-like soils. Clay's water retention gets worse when placed in containers and could cause root decay.

Most vegetables require sunlight. The best chance of a successful tomato harvest if you're cultivating it on a window that faces south and receives a few hours of sunshine each day. They are usually grown in direct sunlight, which means burning them poses a minimal chance. Others, like spinach, require lesser exposure to direct sunlight. Plant them in shade. If you're using pots for your plants It's simple to put your plants under different climates.

No matter if your plants sit outside, or kept inside, insects will be able to be able to reach the plants. Install a screen for insects like you would your outdoor garden. Larvae could grow in container soils if the eggs were laid on the soil prior to being planted. If used according to guidelines, insecticide soaps as well as other commercial mixes are appropriate for handling plants and safe for use when eating the plants.

Fresh vegetables that are readily available offers convenience and secure food choices. Although container gardening requires some effort, the results and dedication are definitely enough to reap the benefits.

Planting vegetables and fruits using containers is a breeze even for beginners or if you don't have an extensive backyard, it could be an excellent idea. There are a variety of veggies that can be grown using this method, such as the eggplant, green onions, cucumbers, cabbage as well as green beans and tomatoes. They are among the vegetables most commonly planted. Many of these climbers, so supports such as wooden posts and trellis, or wire cages may be needed. Containers are able to be placed in balconies, patios or any other dry, arid area.

What kinds of vegetables can you be grown in pots?

It's impossible to plant all of these plants in containers so you'll need to choose small varieties. They are commonly referred to "mini veg" or defined as "appropriate for close spacing." When it comes to beans, select a variety such as Hestia or Sutton and the Sutton for Balconi, Patio, Sweet 1000 or Tiny Tim tomatoes. The most popular is California Wonder Peppers, and Minnesota Midget Melons. Consider Little Gem, and Tom Thumb for salads. They all require less space than conventional varieties, which are specifically created to be grown in tight areas.

Which type of container should you choose?

You can use nearly any container. Just make sure it's large enough, and that it has ample drainage holes. Hanging baskets are another option, as other varieties of tomatoes do very easily. Terracotta pots look beautiful, but need more attention than plastic pots as they tend to dry faster. If you can, choose an earthy-colored one since it's cooler during the summer months and can hold more heat than dark-colored ones in order to prevent the soil from heating rapidly. For water conservation, you can you can use a drip tray underneath the pots.

Which locations are suitable for containers for vegetables?

It is possible to place the pots on your patio or balcony however, make sure that they're to be exposed to heat throughout the day. For vegetables to grow properly, they require a minimum of six hours of sunlight a day. For colder climates, putting the pots against a wall that faces to the south is an excellent option. It is also possible to put the pots on a mobile base that allows you to rotate them to receive sunshine from all directions which will result in an evener growth pattern and also permit you to take away from the sun during the hottest part of the day.

How can you prepare your vegetable garden?

It is essential to choose an excellent quality potting soil. If you want to grow your container, normal gardening soil isn't recommended as it doesn't have an appropriate balance of nutrients and could contain pests as well as seeds of weeds. It is possible to purchase the veggies as young plant transplants or grow seeds indoors or inside the greenhouse. Put a little mulch over the soil up until they're transferred to the pots in order to keep humidity. It is possible to utilize straw or mold for the roots. Be sure not to crowd your seedlings. leave them ample space for growth and build an area where they are able to be able to climb, if needed.

What is the cost to supply water for your container of vegetables?

A majority of pots will need to be watered each day. You could spray three to 4 times per week to the soil with a lower nutrient. Avoid spraying directly on the plants since spraying directly onto leaves can cause the growth of mold and fungi at the base of the plant. Make sure that the pots don't become wet, but ensure that the drainage system is adequate.

It's fun to plant vegetables in containers, and it's extremely easy for even the beginner gardener. After you've picked your bounty of vegetables that are fresh and prepared to cook, or mix into salads You'll surely be rewarded.

How do you create the Elevated Bed Vegetable Garden

If you're planning to build an elevated garden for your vegetables There are a few important points to be aware of. Garden layout is of paramount importance to think about.

Most gardeners who are first timers also fall into the trap of creating an area that's less manageable as they first thought. By utilizing the correct quantity of water, nutrients and sunlight, picking the ideal arrangement for your raised beds can mean less effort for you and more advantages for the vegetables you grow. It all depends on the addition of a few other things and here are the basics to assist you in creating the ideal layout.

Making plans ahead is the very first thing you need to consider, and is it is the first thing to consider considerations when you are thinking of having the garden of your dreams on an elevated bed. It is important to ensure it's set up correctly in order that, when you need to expand it there is no need change things about. If you've left enough space to grow, you may extend further. The available space. Therefore, you have consider which veggies you would like to plant.

There are many benefits to having separate containers for each vegetable. It's something that you'll need be aware of when designing your garden. For each vegetable, the reason to use different containers is because some require specific care (this is why you'll want to have different boxes to protect the most vulnerable plants).

Another thing that you must not forget is picking the best place for your bed. In whatever size mattress you choose to use is important to choose the ideal position. A good position will have:

* Clean ground

* Most sunlight

• Good air circulation. It is important to stay clear of beds which are too large and a high bed difficult to maintain. It is recommended to have approximately 4 feet in length in your garden's raised beds. It means access from the two sides should be relatively simple.

It is important to ensure that your taller plants are in the rear when you plant the raised beds. The reason behind this is because these plants will not interfere with sunlight reaching the smaller ones.

It's an absolute blast building your own raised vegetable garden. So, keeping these suggestions in mind can ensure that your raised bed garden will be an absolute success and thrilling for all those involved. In the near future you'll be reaping the rewards from having your own garden gardens set up in your own backyard.

What issues can be addressed by an elevated bed for vegetable gardens?

There are many people who are concerned about the growth of their veggies. They've heard of various kinds of garden styles and want an information source to assist them start growing their own vegetable gardens without much difficulty. The first question that you could think about is: What are the challenges of running a raised-bed vegetable garden? We'll look at some most common issues faced by gardeners and the solutions that are possible with these kinds of.

Chapter 10: Common Vegetable Gardening Problems

When it comes to getting a an established vegetable garden people who wish to plant their own vegetables face the following four problems. These are related to:

1. Space related issues

2. Poor soil quality

3. Problems with drainage

4. Accessibility concerns

After we have a better understanding of the four main issues vegetable gardeners must deal with, let's try to figure out how we are able to solve them all. The challenge of cultivating vegetables can be summarized in the creation of an elevated vegetable gardening space for people who have to confront these difficulties.

Space-related issues The majority of people reside in urban blocks, subdivisions or even city areas that look like they have a small space within their gardens. It is possible to grow enough veggies to use at home in an elevated garden above ground with only a small amount of space that is. The garden bed of two feet wide by 10 feet is likely to produce enough veggies for the family.

Poor soil It is common to find areas where there is excess clay or sand as well as others with enough or sufficient naturally occurring soil nutrients for them to thrive properly, such as the alkaline. When you have a raised-bed vegetable garden, vegetation is above the ground and you choose the soil mixture from that the bed will be filled with. In addition to other soil mix that you could also add organic gardening materials.

Problems with drainage A lot of yards do not drain properly. If you try to cultivate your own veggies in soil that's poorly draining could reduce the amount of oxygen they require for their survival. In addition, poor drainage could contribute to the development of disease because of the overly fertile soil which could harm the plants. Since the plants are above the ground and have appropriate drainage outlets when you make the bed using a raised bed for your garden will eliminate the problem.

Accessibility concerns - access to the plants they plant could be a problem for certain people. Garden beds that have been elevated are constructed on pedestals that are completely off the ground to ensure that the bed's height is able to allow for a wide range of people without needing to bend or kneel as the typical garden requires. This can be beneficial to those physically challenged that are keen on growing vegetables, but aren't capable of doing so previously but now have the ability to access their garden. This type of gardening it is also possible to not be required to stroll through rows, so tending to or harvesting your plants is just a small distance to the side.

There are a few of issues raised beds for vegetable gardens is able to overcome. Many gardeners are using the raised bed garden is gaining popularity. It's a cost-effective way to plant your own veggies and is a great way to be involved. Once you've figured out your problems raised vegetable garden can resolve and solve, shouldn't it be appropriate to invest in one?

Modern vegetable gardens require an enormous amount of maintenance and work such as feeding, weeding and strict schedules for planting. Also, there is the seasonal problem that allows the gardens to lay down during winter months with no production whatsoever. We are instead instructed to cultivate crops using manure green, and use inorganic fertilisers and chemical to enhance the soil's quality. It requires lots of time, effort and commitment to the whole year round use of the traditional method for growing food yourself.

Is it really necessary to be that difficult?

Ask me the following query. Do forests need to consider what it can do to improve its growth? Do they need to rotate the soil each season? Do you think anyone will come by each time and collect measurements of pH or plants seeds? Will it be able to spray or weed harmful chemical?

Absolutely no!

Modern techniques of vegetable gardening focus on challenges. Did you know that many gardening books are filled with of suggestions for solving issues? In the past I was a typical gardener, and noticed that the solutions for most problems in fact created an entirely new set of issues. The difficulty with this is that it causes additional difficulties.

We'll look at one common tradition of gardening that I'll demonstrate the way in which one issue can turn to a myriad of challenges.

Imagine a typical vegetable garden that is planted with rows of various vegetables. The bare patches of the vegetable garden can be fairly big. The bare spot to the common gardener is just the bare patches. However, a patch that is bare an empty area, to an ecologist, is an unfilled niche that could be an opportunity for creatures from other species to settle in. Nature is not a fan of space that is empty and weeds can be the most efficient fillers in the niche. It is a matter of ecology, and that is exactly what a weed can be the filler of niches. They are the plants that can have a very high degree of colonization. They would not be "weeds" if they weren't.

We're back on our plan. The weeds are growing in gaps. Most of the time, there are too many plants need to be removed in isolation, which is why the common gardener utilizes a hoe push them down into the soil. In a variety of gardening guides and even organic gardening guides I've heard that your hoe can be the best tool you have. Therefore, the message gets us is that a hoe can solve problems.

In this article, I will explain the ways in which a hoe can be in fact causing a whole new problem. First, the act of turning soil stimulates plants that grow weeds, and creates an explosion of weeds. In the second place, turning can disrupt the ecology of the soil. In general, the surface layer of soil is lacking structure and is dry. When you turn it upwards to the top, you can put more well-organized soil over the top and underneath the unstructured soil The area of soil without structure increased in size over the course of time. The soil that is structureless has less capacity to store moisture so the garden requires more water for the plants to stay alive.

In addition, a non-structural soil is unable to pass nutrients to plants in the same way as. It is essential that the garden utilize fertilizer as of now. The majority of fertilizers harm the soil's biology. This is essential to build soil structure as well as the source of nutrients to plants. The soil eventually becomes an unproductive material and doesn't contain the necessary balance of nutrients to create fully developed food items. Diets would, in the end, lack nutrients and vitamins. The issue has been discussed within modern agriculture. According to Dr. Tim Lobstein, Food Commission Director, "Agriculture today does not require the soil to enrich itself, but depends on artificial fertilizers that do not substitute the large range of nutrient plants and human needs." In the last 60 years, the commercially-produced foods have seen significant nutritional and mineral content decreases."

Do you recognize that we started with the problem of weeds but then ended up facing issues of a less capacity to keep water as well as infertile soils? Then, there is an issue that could be serious, increasing low-nutrient food items. The modern gardening techniques often aim only to fix the issue and not solve the root of the issue.

However, there is a solution! It is necessary to employ an approach that blends the ecology of plants, pests soil ecology, the management of crops into a plan that tackles the root of these issues. This method should be effective to make a profit. It must, however, produce sufficient foods to be competitive with traditional methods, in a given location.

Over the past several years I've been looking into ways to grow organically-based food. The method uses no tillage and pesticides. It also produces minimal weeds and only less physical exertion (compared the conventional method of cultivating vegetables). The method also yields many times more food per square meter and can provide food for every day throughout the year.

My garden is modeled after the natural world in a manner that the garden appears like the natural ecosystem, and functions as if it were. The success layering of plants (as you see in nature ecosystems) allows for efficient management of a variety of maladies. Additionally, it removes, obviously, the requirement to rotate crops and rest beds as well as manure plants that are green. The approach to conservation of soil is an organic way, and as a result, each year the soil's structure and fertility the soil gets better and more fertile. Another benefit to this approach is that it automatically seeds renewal. This happens naturally when dormant seeds sprout; and With attractive plants filling empty areas, not the weeds that are common.

The biggest obstacle for this method is to convince gardeners who are not familiar with the advantages. The industry of gardening, as with many other industries, is entangled by an established method. Ecologically-based practices require so very little involvement from humans that people be, to my mind, be frustrated by the lack of a need to observe the activities. Naturally, humans like to control their lives. But by following this way the natural world is allowed to control the situation. This test is for confidence in natural laws which are fundamental. These natural laws can be 100% accurate according to my personal experience.

The most common reason why gardeners dislike this method is because it dispels the mystery of being an professional. The reason is that this approach is simple enough that anybody can use this at any time and anywhere around the globe. Even for seasoned gardeners and a shrewdly simple answer is offered the result can quite dangerous.

It is clear that this is how we'll make food in the coming years. This is just basic logic. So why wouldn't we employ the same system that takes a small less effort producing a number of times more food? It will surely take some time to convince the public that growing food is easy and simple, however those who are willing to accept this approach by a patient explanation and patience.

Clever Ways to Achieve Natural Pest Control in Your Vegetable Garden

If you're unable to manage the plethora of chemical compounds that are a part of your garden, your gardening task is a lot more difficult. But it doesn't need to be this way. If you're someone who is a gardener that likes things to be ordinary and enjoys playing using non-traditional ways of conserving your crop you can find some practical alternatives available.

Designing a variety of products for natural pest control takes only a few minutes, putting involved in the appropriate counter-predatory actions as well as using natural solutions to solve your issue. You'll need patience as well as some kind of joy to observe the ways nature can be utilized to solve many of the problems it brings about.

We'll start with an insect that isn't a problem for the plants as often as it can make you work hard in the scorching hot summer heat weeding or digging up the greenhouse. This is talking about wasps and flies naturally. However, gardeners don't have to worry as over their own personal issues even if they were not too detrimental to their gardens. Help is available with an ingenuous idea for the form of a simple trap for wasps that could also be made using old soda bottles. You'll need a couple of clear plastic bottles that have labeling removed, and that are filled with a bit of sweet syrup in the base. Every insect will be in a position to resist the sweetness and are completely puzzled about their way through. This is a very popular technique that they create beautiful bottles complete with stands as well as additional requirements for positioning.

Organic pesticides can be found for pests who are not attracted to sweet syrup. They can help you search for natural solutions to control pests. Gardeners have been using diatomaceous earth. Mix it with water and then sprayed all over the landscape, especially on the blooming branches. Diatomaceous earth, which is poisonous, seems to cause a corrosive effect will repel insects that are visiting. One issue is that it will repel insect pests in the garden, such as butterfly and ladybugs.

The natural methods for pest control can also be used with bigger rodents like rabbits. Did you try creating a gardenIng space with a few rabbits? The rabbits believe this is an opportunity to create a feast to feed their consumption. One of the best ways to keep animals like deer and rabbits away from your veggie patches should be using the rabbit or chicken wire cages made of wire. Create an enclosure that can be placed over the vegetable garden and you'll be fine. Growing garlic in the vegetable garden is the best option. A lot of animals don't like the smell and so do people. This is a clever approach to keep animals from entering to feel that there's something delicious available for them.

Chapter 11: Important Tools That Are Useful For Vegetable Gardening

If you're an avid gardener who wants to cultivate your own veggies There are a variety of sources available to assist you in achieving some prize-winning. If you're an experienced vegetable gardener, then you'll understand how important it is to have the best equipment complete the job. When you go out to purchase all the gardening tools for your vegetable patch It's crucial to take into consideration the dimensions of your vegetable patch and your physical capability to perform what gardening demands.

The very first step of vegetable gardening is to lay the area of your garden and till the soil so that it's ready to seed. Particularly, when you have an extensive vegetable garden it could be quite a bit of task. You'll need a range of equipment to help. Forks and spades are the primary two equipment you'll require for the job. A spade can be useful in making a hole in the dirt you've marked to plant your seeds, and the fork is able to split soil into smaller, better-suited chunks, and then include compost in the mixture. If you suspect that you will be having difficulty digging, however you may want to consider buying the growers' equipment or an rotating tiller. A cultivator or rotary tiller does all the hard work of digging your land to make the soil look as you would like.

After you've tilled it then you must start thinking about planting. It's usually a good option to go over your soil using a rake, to level it and make it ready, and sew your seeds is the best option to suit your needs. It is a great idea to arrange your vegetable in groups and allow plenty of space between the sets.

The online sale of seeds for vegetables could be an excellent alternative. Most companies don't pack their seeds ahead of time and allow the seeds to stay fresher longer. Additionally, many retailers deliver the following day, which means that a quick shipping is certain. Also, you can find a diverse selection of seeds which you won't find in your neighborhood retailer. In addition, nurseries or greenhouses don't have an extensive selection of seeds to grow plants. If you're in search of the most sought-after organic tomato seeds, it's likely to search online for it.

The majority of vegetable seed businesses offer an online guarantee. They may offer a refund of the cost of purchase or exchange the seed if it fails to perform in a specified period of time. This is probably the most sought-after kind of warranty will be offered. There are other assurances that say If you're unhappy in any way the company will reimburse the money. Whatever the case, ensure you know the conditions and terms prior to purchasing.

Price ranges are generally very similar and you should look at the prices of a few products before purchasing the item. Check out the quantity you purchase. There are many websites that may be cheaper because they offer a smaller mass. Take note of the price of seeds, and. As an example, the seeds created from heirloom varieties yield the finest tomato tastings. There are a variety of different kinds of the same plant and. Make sure you are comparing with the same type of crop else you'll miss an exact picture.

You should have an idea of the kind of vegetable you would like to plant. Are you looking for a diverse assortment of exotic staples as well as? A few organic veggies are what you are looking for. Perhaps you'd like to have an old-fashioned gardening space with staples for cooking within it? No matter what you choose there's a company that will suit your needs.

You should make sure that you purchase from an established seed business for your vegetables. If you're uncertain which direction to take, inquire with some of your acquaintances for their favorite places to purchase seeds. If you know someone who is a gardener around the block, ask for their source of plants, or if they've got any tips. Another option to learn ideas is to join an online chat room with the gardener on the internet. Gardeners will also provide assistance to anyone in need of advice.

The process of planting a garden for vegetables can be a highly satisfying feeling. Enjoy your garden gardens, but be sure to remember the things we've discussed. The tips you've learned could in the future, will save you time as well as reduce the frustration. Making purchases from a reputable online business can be a cost-effective and simple method to get your garden started.

HOW TO PLANT A FLOWER GARDEN

FOR BEAUTY AND FUNCTION

The lower ones are usually only planted for aesthetics but others could serve an actual purpose. It is important to put much consideration into what the location of your garden ought to be before you make the decision to plant to plant a garden with flowers. It all depends on the space that you have. There may be a need for an "indoor" garden, or hanging a basket placed on the balcony in case you reside in a cramped space. If you are limited in areas, containers are also a good option. The green thumb of yours may be able to take advantage of a tiny plant gardening space. If you're lucky enough possess a large enough outdoor space, then you'll have plenty of possibilities.

Like the variety of plants are in existence, so are various varieties of floral gardens. This should be kept of when planning your garden. Thus, you must begin with a strategy. It is possible to end having a mess to clean up if you select a few plants only to plant them randomly.

The first step is to take a brief review of the area available. Make a sketch of the entire area, including your residence, outbuildings the sources of water, plants and trees, and even non-digging zones like underground cables. Create your diagram at the smallest scale feasible to ensure that you do not come with any surprises, such as the purchase of too many plants that don't be able to fit in your existing area. In your diagram, you could draw circles of trees.

What do you need from the garden? Could it be a spot for you to rest? In order to make up for the lack of sitting area or for an outdoor hammock to nap in? Do you want to install an irrigation system? Make a sketch of the features in your landscape design, and indicate what you'd like them to place them. It may be beneficial to break the space into zones if you are in a large outdoor area with public spaces to host barbecues or family gatherings as well as more exclusive areas to create your personal space.

How long will you be spending in your gardening space? Some flowers and plants require significantly more attention in order in order to be secure as well as beautiful. Pick tougher plants when you are limited in time, and need less time to care for. Plants that require lamps and perennials will need greater care since they must be replaced every year. Certain, they can be grown year-to-year with little effort from you. An important part of gardening involves watching plants thrive in the unique surroundings.

At the entrance of your home or on a pathway or driveway, you may simply want to create an area of flowering plants. When you've got longer time to spare, you could like to plant a larger section of flowers.

While you are preparing your garden be aware of when the flowers is expected to bloom. The spring bulbs, the annuals flowering perennials, and other flowers will are in bloom during the fall. If you plan it correctly it is possible to have things that bloom all three seasons (or at times four).

The more you plan for success, the more successful you'll be in whatever endeavor you choose to pursue. It's much easier to create a plan for your landscape "in your head" than having no plans whatsoever. Once you've come up with your plan, plant and admire the stunning blooms that result from your efforts.

HOW TO GET BEAUTIFUL FLOWERS WITHOUT DAMAGING YOUR BUDGET

Are you wondering how you can give your dear family members beautiful gifts and flowers that won't break your budget? Do you want to find the most economical method to present your loved ones with presents? Do you like the smell and freshness of flowers along with an amazing combination of artistically designed and beautifully arranged flowers that convey your best wishes? With the advancement of access and modern technology, such as online shopping and electronic commerce it is possible to present flowers to people living in different parts of the globe.

It is possible to gift your loved ones gorgeous bouquets and flowers with no cost. Visit the closest flower shop or floral distributors for a start. If they're part of a bigger distribution and take online orders, that's more convenient. It is also possible to select your present online and place your order on the internet, rather than visiting the store. The company can also offer fast and prompt delivery of floral arrangements within their area of service, including delivery the day that orders are made. Online shopping is more efficient because it does not require middlemen's cost. Freshlyarranged flower arrangements are priced based upon the flower varieties you select beginning at $40. There is a wide selection of floral arrangements and hues - rose Ivy, orchids daisy, gerbera asters and dahlia can be picked from a variety of florists. Roses are the most loved flowers for all occasions A stunning heart-shaped flower arrangement comprised of first-class red roses can cost about $300. The cost of the flower that you choose could be greater based on the grade the flowers, their availability and the popularity.

It is obvious that you can could have your own backyard, where the ornamental plants you choose can flourish. Visit the closest nursery to choose the flower that you want to incorporate into the gift. You can learn to cultivate them at the nursery and when of the year they'll bloom. Flowers are produced by plants throughout the year, with there are some that bloom in one season, and some blooming throughout the year. Make sure you include types of orchids, including gardens roses, anthurium as well as other decorative green plants you can find within your garden. A plastic wrapper that has light-colored designs with ribbons, a clear tape can be used to design your own personalized gift. It is also possible to purchase smaller size stickers or cards on which you could make a note or write your own message. You can also use heart-shaped buns that let you beautifully put together the bouquet.

You can now start saying things using flowers. It's all at reasonable costs, but without breaking the budget.

PROBLEMS GROWING FLOWERS

Even in the most well-cared for gardens, things can happen and it's ridiculous to believe that disease and pests just attack plants with a sick condition. Be vigilant to defend your garden from outside intruders, no matter how beautiful your borders and beds appear, since there are pests as well as fungal diseases that can cause destruction to your plants and ruin the efforts you put into. Plants are most susceptible to being afflicted by an enemy from within instead of through an external invader. These internal reasons could include the poor condition the soil you have, a lack of water, food and wind. You may also experience frost or you choose the wrong plants or choose something wrong. Prior to the problem starts the best way to ensure maintaining healthy plants is to stay clear of trouble and then deal with it swiftly when it becomes apparent.

Avoid trouble when choosing. If you purchase a quality selection, it will not work in the right spot. The styles of Evite are fragile for your garden. Do not plant any annuals that like shade or sun like in the shade of trees. Your spectacle is probably going to disappoint.

Prepare the area thoroughly. Strong-growing plants are far more likely than an inexperienced plant to recover from a epidemic or attack of disease. Waterlogging is among the biggest problems encountered in clayey soils because of poor soil preparation. If you are planning to plant perennials, you must get rid of all roots that are causing weeds and then apply Bromophos onto the soil, if rodents are chewing roots in other areas of the garden.

Sow or plant according to the time of year. Seed sowing is about taking the proper steps in the appropriate timeframe If you plant too early in the outdoors seedlings will turn brown, plant too late and the result will be only of a limited lifespan. Once the seed has been sow indoors, be aware the fact that "hardening" is necessary before the seeds can be moved outside.

www.ingramcontent.com/pod-product-compliance
Lightning Source LLC
Chambersburg PA
CBHW070734020526
44118CB00035B/1352